THE SOMME
THEN AND NOW

This book is dedicated to the memory of the many thousands of men who became part of Kitchener's New Army and met their destiny on the battlefields of Picardy.

THE SOMME
THEN AND NOW

JOHN GILES

AN
AFTER THE BATTLE
PUBLICATION

AFTER THE BATTLE

THE SOMME — THEN AND NOW

© John Giles 1986
First published by Bailey Brothers and Swinfen Ltd in 1977.

This revised edition published in 1986 on the 70th anniversary of the first day of the battle — 1st July — by Battle of Britain Prints International Ltd., Church House, Church Street, London E15 3JA, England.
Reprinted 1991

Printed in Great Britain by
Plaistow Press Limited,
Church House, Church Street,
London E15 3JA

ISBN: 0 900913 41 X

FRONT COVER
The best preserved trench memorial on the Somme — Beaumont Hamel Newfoundland Memorial Park. (See pages 15 and 16.)

REAR COVER
The memorial cross on the crown of the Butte de Warlencourt with the village of Le Sars in the valley below.

FRONT ENDPAPER
Left: Troops of the Gordon Highlanders in a support trench near Nesle on the 20th Division Front, 24th March 1918.

Right: Wounded British soldier obviously relieved to be out of the fighting with a 'Blighty' wound is carried to the rear by German prisoners near Ginchy, during the battle of Flers-Courcelette on 15th September 1916.

REAR ENDPAPER
Left: German prisoners are marched to a PoW cage near Amiens, watched by relaxed British, Australian and American troops on 9th August 1918.

Right: A man and his steed. The pathetic remains of a German cavalryman and horse which was photographed near Villers-Bretonneaux on 18th August 1918.

FRONTISPIECE
A wounded and bewildered German soldier receives first aid from a British medical orderly near Bernasay Wood on 19th July 1916.

PART 1
The mine going up beneath the Hawthorn Redoubt at 7.20 a.m. on 1st July 1916. It made a crater forty feet deep.

PART 2
A leisurely stroll for one Briton down the shell-scarred Amiens-St. Quentin road on 16th March 1917.

PART 3
A Mark 4 tank passes through the village of Péronne during the battle for St. Quentin on 23rd March 1918. The vulnerability of the horse-mounted cavalry which the tanks were destined to replace is pitifully evident in the foreground.

PART 4
The town of Albert seen from the north-east. The Church of Nôtre-Dame-de-Brebière is in the centre, with the Hotel de Ville and main square below.

CONTENTS

PROLOGUE

More than three-score years have passed since the start of the Battle of the Somme. In the following few hours that fair summer's day of 1st July 1916, over 57,000 British soldiers lay wounded, dying or dead on the chalky uplands of Picardy; and the countryside itself was already a desolation of shattered villages, shell-torn fields and splintered trees. Never before or since have so many British soldiers died in such a moment of time, nor — except at Ypres and Verdun — has such devastation been visited upon one small, fruitful area of earth. By the time the offensive had wallowed to a halt in the November rains, the casualties, among British, French and Germans, had risen to over a million and the land itself was a sodden, sterile wilderness.

Today the sun shines once more on fertile acres and prosperous farms. The flattened villages have been solidly rebuilt; and those stands of riven timber and evil reputation, High Wood, Mametz, Trones and Delville, are peaceful oases of leafy trees where birds nest and sing. Nowadays you have to search for relics of those earlier, grim times — old shells, scraps of barbed wire, the traces of a trench-line or the scar of a mine crater. Already they are one with history, with the arrowheads and earthworks of even older wars, but rather more dangerous.

Occasionally the plough or the bulldozer turn up more personal mementoes, a cap badge, a belt buckle, a soldier's bones. On Thiepval Memorial alone are carved the names of 73,000 men who have no known resting place. Dozens of military cemeteries tell the same story: here, between the River Somme and its modest tributary, the Ancre, between July and November 1916, a generation died.

During the summers of 1971, 1973 and 1974, I spent many weeks there, tracing out the battle-lines, matching against contemporary photographs the spots, each one of unbelievable, heart-breaking heroism, following the shifting boundaries of No Man's Land, identifying the uninterrupted fields of fire of the German machine-gunners which, above all that first deadly morning, rendered inevitable the appalling British casualties. What follows, therefore, is not only an account of the series of engagements that make up the Battle of the Somme, and a view of the battleground as it is today, but a special tribute to the men of Kitchener's New Army, so many of whom lie beneath the soil of France, near the river from which one of history's greatest conflicts obtained its title. It is also an acknowledgement to the tenacity of an enemy who fought bravely to retain his hold on former territorial gains.

JOHN GILES, 1977.

INTRODUCTION TO REVISED EDITION

The well-received first edition of this book went out of print several years ago but demand for a reprint built up steadily, particularly as the 70th anniversary of the bitter Somme battles approached.

The book's formula (identical to my first, *The Ypres Salient*, in 1970) proved very popular as it gave historic details of those tragic yet valiant days and also enabled the reader to visually register places on the old WWI battlefields more easily than through the written word alone. For those who have found it possible to visit those hallowed fields, woods and villages it has proved an invaluable guide to pinpointing specific locations where once fierce battles raged over a period of nearly five months throughout that fateful year of 1916; for a limited time in early 1917, and then again in 1918, in the August of which began the long hard slog to final victory.

The much-valued co-operation of *After the Battle* magazine has made possible the availability of this second edition, to which has been added an extra section (Part 4) that presents the battlefield as it is today, using recent aerial photographs. Together with the inclusion of illustrations of many relics I have come across during my visits, it is felt that these will give an additional interest to many people, coupled with a wider perspective of the battlefields generally.

Little has changed in the Somme area since the 1970s. Some new houses have been erected but generally the villages and countryside remain much the same as they were then — quiet backwaters, by-passed by the fast moving and heavy motorway traffic on the eastern edge of the battlefields, near Bapaume.

JOHN GILES, 1986

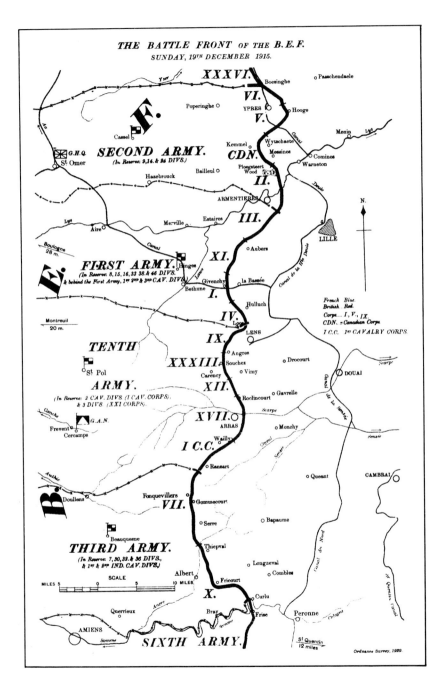

LIST OF MAPS

THE PLAN AND PREPARATIONS

On 6th December 1915, during an Allied military conference at the Chantilly headquarters of General Joffre, the French C-in-C, tentative plans were laid for a major offensive by the French, with the close support of British forces, on a front of approximately fifty miles astride the Somme. This was to be yet another attempt — the first with full co-ordination between the French and British — to breach the Germans' defences and to bring to an end the frustrations of trench warfare. All previous ones, by either side, had failed, with heavy loss of life and derisory gains of ground, including the British offensives at Neuve Chapelle and Loos earlier in the year. The area which Joffre had chosen for this new push stretched from south of the Somme to north of the Ancre; open, rolling, chalk-based country, containing some of the most heavily fortified villages on the whole of the Western Front, and a formidable defence system constructed by the Germans during the previous two years. Vast belts of barbed wire, well-sited machine-gun posts, a complex trench network — and, as was learnt too late, deep shelters which were virtually indestructible — comprised a series of obstacles of almost unassailable strength. Add to this the fact that all along the line from Gommecourt in the north to Fricourt in the south and some distance eastwards, the enemy occupied the higher ground with first-class troops, and the full burden of the attackers' task can be appreciated.

The Commander-in-Chief of the British Expeditionary Force, General Sir Douglas Haig, who had recently superseded Sir John French, would have preferred the new offensive to take place in Flanders, where he envisaged rolling up the German right flank and thereby clearing the Channel ports; but 'Papa' Joffre had his way, and in February 1916 the French plan was adopted. With nearly 40 divisions, they were to bear the brunt of the assault, mainly south of the Somme, while the British sector covered a front of about 18 miles, joining the French at Maricourt. But, on 21st February, the enemy launched an offensive of his own, directed towards Verdun; an offensive that was to suck into its terrible battles more and more French divisions, burn into the French memory the name Verdun as the Somme and Passchendaele were branded into the British, and, eventually, leave only five of their divisions to take part in the first stage of the new Allied assault that summer.

Accordingly, the roles of the two allies became reversed, with the main burden now transferred to 13 British divisions. And, as the bitter and costly struggle in front of Verdun ground on, Joffre became more and more insistent on rapid help from his ally. The opening date of the Somme offensive was brought forward from 1st July to 25th June — though it was later postponed to the original date — and preparations for it went ahead at top speed. Vast dumps of stores and ammunition were assembled behind the lines; new railways built, bridges strengthened, roads constructed; miles of water pipes were laid, and the whole area around Albert seethed with activity. All of it clearly visible to the Germans in their excellent observation posts on the high ground overlooking the town.

As if the evidence of their own eyes was not enough to alert the enemy, French newspapers took care to report a coming British offensive, and British munition workers were publicly invited to forego their Whitsun holiday until the end of July. In spite of all this, the German C-in-C, General Erich von Falkenhayn at first refused to believe that the attack would come on the Somme with its elaborate defences; doubts that were shared by Crown Prince Rupprecht, but which were dispersed when the veteran French XX ('Iron') Corps moved into the line south of the Somme. Any that remained vanished when, at 6 am on the 24th June, the British bombardment from over 1,400 guns began, and continued for the next seven days and nights, swamping — it was supposed — the German defences with 1½ million shells. Meanwhile, in the air above, the RFC traversed far and wide, spotting for the guns and taking photographs; and beneath the ground, miners worked their long silent tunnels under the German lines.

Imperial War Museum

By 1st July, General Rawlinson's Fourth Army consisted of over half a million men, the great majority of them Kitchener volunteers and Territorials; of whom 100,000 were to go over the top in the first assault. On their left, the 46th (North Midland) and 56th (London) Divisions, from VII Corps of General Allenby's Third Army, were to make a subsidiary attack on the major enemy salient at Gommecourt. Allenby himself would have preferred a much heavier diversionary attack farther north, but was overruled by Haig.

Above: General Sir Douglas Haig, with General Joffre (left) and General Foch, leaving the British Commander-in-Chief's Chateau at Beauquesne (north of Amiens), 12th August 1916, after luncheon with His Majesty King George Vth.

Haig's principal objective was to break through the enemy defences and then roll up their line eastward and northward by utilising cavalry under the command of General Gough. It was hoped that the enemy's second line would be reached on the first day, and perhaps even successfully broken. His aim, in fact, was for a quick, decisive result; yet it is known that he was prepared for a long, hard fight, and his Chief Intelligence Officer, Brigadier General Charteris noted in his diary that the battle was likely to be one of attrition, and heavy casualties were to be expected.

The French, who were now into their fourth month of this very process before Verdun, consoled themselves with the thought that attrition works for both sides, for and against. The more the enemy were worn down and weakened, the sooner would he be ejected from the sacred soil of France; and if the British attack on the Somme drew off some of the German reserves from the Meuse, so much the better. It must never be forgotten, when considering the tragedy of the Somme, that French soldiers had been fighting desperately and with incredible courage for four long months to hold back the German masses hurled against them at Verdun.

Meanwhile, in the British lines from Gommecourt to Maricourt, tension grew. As the preliminary bombardment continued — and, many wondered, with hope born of dread, could any living thing survive such a battering — Haig moved up from his headquarters at Montreuil to Beauquesne and Rawlinson to Querrieu Chateau, about 12 miles behind the trenches. For a great many of their soldiers, inexperienced and, indeed, half-trained, this was to be their baptism of fire; yet their morale was high, their main objective was to get to grips with the enemy. In this laudable intention, considerable numbers were to be cheated by death or wounds.

Above: **Men of the Border Regiment in a front line trench, Thiepval Wood, 1916.**
Below: **A group of German soldiers outside their dug-out. Enemy trenches were invariably more solidly constructed and often contained deep shelters.**

Above: German trenches at La Boisselle undergoing bombardment by British artillery before the offensive. (Compare this picture with photographs of the same area on pages 29-31).

The horizon ahead, in the growing darkness, appears to be lit up by fires. A red glow hangs on the skyline caused by the continual explosion of shells from the British bombardment. The German positions must be dreadful with those continual waves of bursting explosive. How anyone can survive is a mystery.

Giles Eyre

Above: An airman's viewpoint of the battlefield at the southern end of the line. The triangular wood left of centre is Fricourt Wood, with the remains of Fricourt on the near side. The dark mass of Mametz Wood is beyond and, jutting into the top left-hand portion above it, is part of High Wood. Flers lies slightly above and to the right of the latter. Over on the extreme right is Delville Wood, with the buildings of Longueval being faintly discernible in front of the trees.

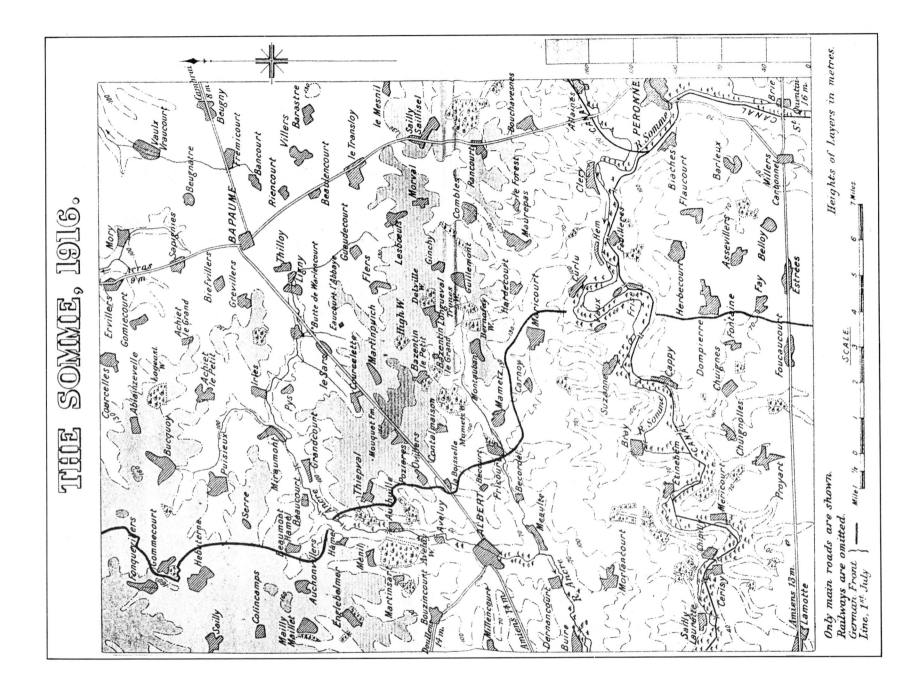

THE SOMME, 1916.

Only main roads are shown.
Railways are omitted.
German Front
Line, 1st July

SCALE.

Heights of layers in metres.

A TOWN CALLED

ALBERT

The strategic importance of Albert was similar to that of Ypres, at the northern end of the British front, for, as with the latter town, it was the hub of a road network with supply-line arteries radiating to the nearby battle zone. A main railway linked it with the major base of Amiens, about fourteen miles away, and it was also served by the old Roman Amiens-Bapaume highway, which was cut by the enemy trenches a short distance east of the town.

With the aid of telescopes and binoculars the enemy enjoyed observation advantage, and systematically bombarded the town which was reduced to heaps of jumbled ruins. The Church of Nôtre-Dame-de-Brebière (incorrectly described by British troops as a Cathedral) became a target for the gunners and, in mid-June 1915, a shell exploded close to the base of the gilded statue of the Virgin with the infant Jesus outstretched in her arms. The statue did not fall completely, but leaned over precariously at an angle of about fifteen degrees below the horizontal, thus creating a legend that when the Virgin fell the war would end. However, French engineers fixed the statue with wire cables which helped to make it reasonably secure.

During the war the 'Leaning Virgin' became a major landmark of the Somme battlefields, and considerable numbers of our troops passed beneath it on their way to the front.

In the severe fighting of March 1918, both statue and church were totally destroyed. Rebuilding took place between 1927 and 1929.

We trudge through the dark, rubble-covered streets of Albert, half unreal in the darkness, and out beyond, the rain now beating at us and running down in riverlets from our ground sheets, draped round shoulders and heads. The rumble of the guns is now strong, and a strange rosy glare lights the sky where it merges with the ground beyond. We are entering the immediate back area of the battle-line, and dumps, trucks, railway lines and occasional hastily-filled shell-holes are much in evidence. The gleam of candles here and there betokens shelters. Gangs of men pass by loaded with stores, and a sudden noisy crash, followed by the swish of speeding shells, marks the heavy battery positions.

Giles Eyre

Imperial War Museum

Above: The ruins of the Church of Nôtre-Dame-de-Brebière, with the 'Leaning Virgin' at the top, September, 1916.

Imperial War Museum

Above: 'Still' from the official film 'The Somme', showing a cheerful group of Tommies moving up to the battle zone. Two men in the middle are carrying Lewis Guns, (light machine-guns).

A relic of the battle unearthed over half a century later.

(Map from the Official History — see acknowledgements)
The above sketch map also details numbers and general dispositions of divisions at the opening of the battle on 1st July, excluding the diversionary attack sector of the 46th and 56th Divisions in the extreme north. No attack was planned for that portion of the line held by units of the 48th (South Midland) Division, although two battalions of that division went into action on the 4th Division's front and suffered numerous casualties. Opposite Fricourt the 50th Brigade of 17th Division was in the line attached to 21st Division; the remainder of the former division was in reserve. Other reserves are indicated behind the front line formations. Additionally, three divisions of cavalry were stationed behind the front awaiting an opportunity to exploit a breakthrough.

28th June (1916)

My own beloved wife

We are on the eve of a great action in which A has been detailed to take a dangerous part in fact the 8th Bde was specially selected for it.

I am writing this now in case I do not come out of it. Dearest you have been the best wife a man could have had and I was very lucky to have won you. I have always loved you only and our short married life was very happy.

The money affairs stand at Cox's, the National Bank of India London & Bombay. I don't think that there is anything at Pindi. There are also 100 Shares Bradford Dyers, 20£ in the War loan a 150£ in premium bonds. The life insurance is in the standard. You will also get a pension for yourself and the "Brat". I am afraid you will be badly off but as you know our income has not admitted of much saving.

Give my ring to Suzanne and give my mother something of mine anything she should care for that you like to give.

I hope if I go out I shall go decently & do my duty manfully, well before doing so.

God keep you dearest
ever your loving husband
George

To be forwarded in care of my death only GFF.

Mrs Farran
121 Bushy Pk Road
Rathgar
Dublin

"IN THE EVENT OF MY DEATH"

Copy of a moving letter from Major G. F. Farran, Royal Field Artillery, written shortly before the commencement of the Somme offensive. He survived the first two weeks of the assault but was killed on 18th July while on duty in an artillery observation post in Bailiff Wood, near Contalmaison.

Major Farran, who was thirty-four years old and a Regular soldier, was buried in Becourt Military Cemetery, just behind the old front line. Later his widow received a touching letter from his former batman, Gunner M. Hodges, in which the latter spoke of the major as being one "for whom I had the deepest affection and respect".

In his letter the Major refers to the 'Brat', which was an affectionate term for his three-year-old daughter, Suzanne, to whom he left his ring. She was the wife of the late Lieut.-Col. G. C. Bloxam, O.B.E., of Lympne, Hythe, Kent.

Four days before his actual death Major Farran wrote another letter in the pages of an army notebook. This, and some photographs, appear further on in this book.

PART 1

THE ATTACK IS LAUNCHED
- Fonquevillers and Gommecourt
- Serre (including 'A Day to Remember')
- Beaumont Hamel
- Newfoundland Memorial Park
- Beaucourt Hamel and The Ancre
- Thiepval, Schwaben Redoubt and Leipzig Redoubt
- Ovillers-la-Boisselle and La Boisselle
- Fricourt
- Mametz
- Carnoy and Montauban
- Casualties of 1st July

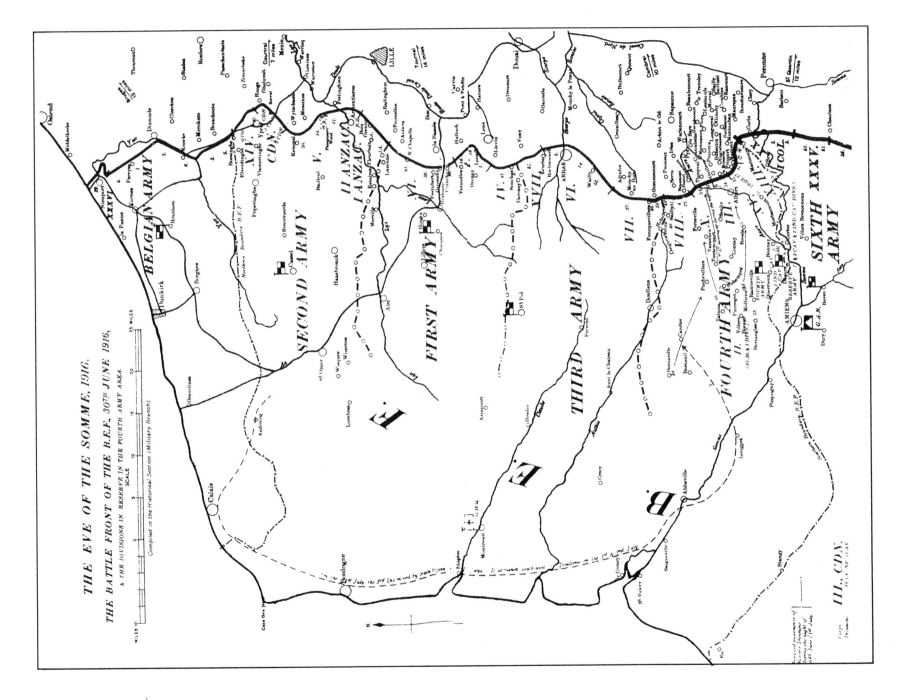

THE EVE OF THE SOMME, 1916.

THE BATTLE FRONT OF THE B.E.F., 30TH JUNE 1916,
& THE DIVISIONS IN RESERVE IN THE FOURTH ARMY AREA.

SCALE

Compiled in the Historical Section (Military Branch)

THE ATTACK IS LAUNCHED

At 7.20 a.m. on the 1st July, ten minutes before zero hour, the huge mine that had been laboriously placed beneath the German redoubt at Beaumont Hamel was exploded, thereby warning the enemy that attack was imminent. Eight minutes later, the remaining eighteen mines were fired (with, in one case, a delayed explosion occurring because of a fault), and the artillery increased their range to hammer the enemy support lines. At 7.30 a.m. precisely, whistles blew all along the British front, and the first assault waves scrambled out of their trenches. The Battle of the Somme had begun.

Above: The old mine crater at Beaumont Hamel today, from the same position as the war-time photograph.

As the artillery barrage lifted from the enemy front line trenches — the creeping barrage was not yet a standard feature of infantry attacks — and the guns increased their range to pound the rear supports, the Germans rushed up from their underground shelters. Immediately their front line was fully manned, with numerous machine-guns sited in the remains of trenches and convenient shell-holes.

From behind their sights they watched the leading masses of British soldiers, rank upon rank in extended lines, moving slowly forward towards them, rifles at the port, as if there was nothing left for them to do except to keep on walking, over cut wire and obliterated trenches, through to the back areas. This was how they had been trained; and since each man was carrying over sixty-six pounds of equipment, and for most of them the advance was uphill, they had no option but to walk. Only in one or two instances that morning was any attempt made to improve upon this leisurely method of attack, notably by the French veterans, who advanced in short rushes, using whatever cover was available.

The British, for the most part, came steadily on. Then, as the German counter-barrage crashed down, the hidden machine-guns opened up, and every German soldier began to blaze away with his rifle, some, in their excitement, kneeling on the parapet or standing up, to get a better field of fire; and the lines of khaki-clad soldiers simply withered away. The shells rained down upon No Man's Land and upon the British trenches; cutting off the leading waves — or what remained of them — and decimating those that followed almost before they started. Some of the German machine-gunners concentrated their fire on the paths which had been cut in our own wire, and soon they were piled high with the dead and dying. Here and there our men reached the enemy's trenches; but more often than not the British barrage had failed to cut the dense thickets of the enemy wire, and men died in their hundreds trying to find a way through. Very soon No Man's Land was a slaughter-yard, with the wounded screaming among the mutilated bodies of the dead, and our own trenches were choked with casualties as the German artillery intensified their barrage in their determination to smash the attack in its infancy.

By mid-day this aim had been largely achieved; and with one or two exceptions, our troops were back in their own trenches or lying dead or wounded in No Man's Land. The few who had succeeded in penetrating beyond the enemy's first lines had been, almost without exception, cut off and either taken prisoner or killed. Only on the right flank were objectives reached and held.

As the sun went down on that first, disastrous day of July 1916, the magnitude of the tragedy had still to be appreciated by those in command; and it was several days before the casualty returns brought home to them the inescapable truth, that the British Army in France had met with a major defeat. Before that realisation, orders had been issued for a continuance of the assault; orders that were to condemn both sides to a long drawn out battle of attrition, lasting almost five months.

With the separate engagements which marked that fluctuating and bloody struggle — Albert, Bazentin Ridge, Delville Wood, Pozières Ridge, Guillemont, Ginchy, Thiepval and the rest — we shall be dealing in due course. First, we must examine in more detail the fighting on that first day, following the line from north to south, and then along to our junction with the French.

Imperial War Museum

Above: German heavy machine-gun with its crew, waiting to go into action. It was these guns that caused such heavy losses during the initial assault .

An old soldier's souvenirs of his time on the battlefields of France. German helmet still bearing its hand painted camouflage and belt taken from one of the fatherland's sons who had no further use for them.

VII CORPS (Lieut.-Gen. Sir T. D ' O Snow) of THIRD ARMY, commanded by
General Sir E. Allenby.

46th (North Midland) Division (Maj.-Gen. Hon. Montagu Stuart-Wortley).
Territorial Division

56th (London) Division. (Maj.-Gen. C. P. A. Hull)
Territorial Division

FONQUEVILLERS AND GOMMECOURT

The village of Fonquevillers, known by the troops as 'Funky-villers', lay just to the rear of the British front line, almost opposite the Gommecourt salient, and was the northernmost point of attack. The principal aim of the 46th Division, who had been stationed here for almost a year, and the 56th Division on their right, was to create a diversion, and so occupy the attention of enemy troops whose fire power might have been used against the Fourth Army's left flank at Serre, a few miles further south.

These divisions were to attack north and south of the salient and, by a pincer movement, endeavour to link up behind Gommecourt and thereby outflank that heavily fortified village.

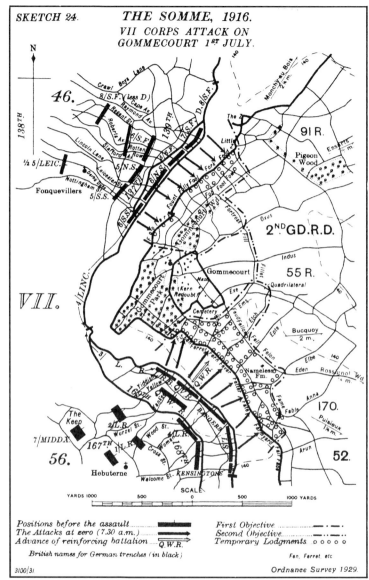

Sketch map from 'Official History Of The War

Imperial War Museum

Left: British shells bursting on German trenches opposite Fonquevillers (Foncquevillers), July, 1916. Note the rum jar in the foreground.

3

Before the assault, men of the 46th Division had already undergone severe trials in trenches that were half filled with water from the heavy rainfalls which, incidently, had been particularly bad at that end of the line. It was there, too, that the mud was at its worst.

At zero hour the 46th attacked in waves and the men quickly found themselves in trouble. Smoke caused confusion and, worst of all, the wire in front of the enemy trenches was found to be mostly uncut. Extremely heavy fire was directed at the attackers and very serious casualties were incurred. Many of the men died in No Man's Land and on the German wire.

Within a short time the assault had fizzled out in that portion of the line and the very few British soldiers who had desperately fought their way through the German first position were cut off and destroyed.

At the southern end of the salient the situation was at first much more encouraging. There the 56th Division had dug a new trench in No Man's Land from which they emerged at zero hour with, in consequence, less distance to travel in order to reach the German trenches. Four battalions attacked vigorously and succeeded in overrunning the enemy front line defences. Other successes followed and for a time it looked as if all would go well with the assault.

However, the enemy quickly recovered from his initial setback and immediately the failure in the north became apparent he devoted most of his attention and fire power to ousting the 56th Division from its gains. Firstly he brought down a terrible barrage on No Man's Land behind the advanced British troops upon whom he also poured enfilading machine-gun fire. This effectively cut off the attackers and stopped any supports from reaching them.

Above right: Aerial view of German trenches at Gommecourt, with ruins of the village on the left.
Below right: Where the 56th (London) Division assaulted the southern arm of the German defences at Gommecourt. Remnants of trenches can still be seen in the fields, and on the right is a stone-built British defence position.

Various attempts were made to reinforce the beleaguered troops or to replenish their dwindling supplies of grenades and ammunition but this led only to the annihilation of the men who tried to cross the hellish stretch of No Man's Land. Whole companies were wiped out and the ground became strewn with dead and dying.

Fighting valiantly the survivors of the original attacking force held on until fierce enemy pressure and shortage of ammunition gradually compelled them to fall back to the German first line. At dusk the shattered remnants of the battalions returned to their own trenches leaving many dead comrades within the enemy position.

VII Corps suffered something like 7,000 casualties with, at the end of the day (and in spite of the gallantry of the troops), nothing to show for it.

Gommecourt remained in German hands for another eight months until the enemy began the Retreat to the Hindenburg Line. Even at that time — all those months after the attacks — some decomposed bodies from the 46th Division were found on the German wire whilst others were collected from No Man's Land.

Above left: All that remained of the village of Gommecourt and the chateau after the deluge of shells from the British guns. Gommecourt was said to be the most strongly fortified village on the whole Somme front and it certainly lived up to its reputation on 1st July.

Below left: Rebuilt Gommecourt village, with a water tanker passing the church. Lack of water was a major problem during the battle, particularly for the wounded.

Imperial War Museum

VIII CORPS (Lieut.-Gen. Sir A. Hunter Weston), of
FOURTH ARMY commanded by General Sir Henry Rawlinson.

31st Division (Maj.-Gen. R. Wanless O'Gowan) — New Army Division

4th Division (Maj.-Gen. Hon. W. Lambton) — Regular Division

SERRE

The village of Serre was on the left flank of the main Fourth Army attack and was the objective of the 31st Division. This division was comprised mostly of men from Hull, Leeds, Bradford, Accrington, Sheffield, Barnsley and Durham, who were mainly formed into what were known as 'Pals' battalions. This helped to foster a wonderful feeling of comradeship but it possibly also created a deeper sense of loss after these battalions had been hard hit by a high casualty rate.

The 'Pals' attacked courageously on that first day of July but were flailed by machine-gun fire and fell in large numbers before they had crossed No Man's Land. A few reached Serre itself but were wiped out, whilst others lay in heaps in front of the German wire.

The attack on Serre was completely repulsed and the pulverised village did not fall into our hands until the retirement of the Germans to the Hindenburg Line early in 1917.

Slightly to the south, and on the Serre road, is now situated a large British military cemetery (Serre Road Cemetery No.2.) which was once the site of a German redoubt known as the Quadrilateral. This was captured by troops of the 4th Division, who fought over ground between Serre and Beaumont Hamel, but was later abandoned. This division also suffered very heavy losses and whole ranks fell as they crossed No Man's Land.

Above left: Serre after it had been blasted out of existence by the British barrage. This picture was taken following the German retreat in 1917.

Below left: The entrance to Serre today, with, on the right, a crucifix, and on the left, just beyond the building, a memorial to the Sheffield City Battalion.

Serre was a heavily fortified village surrounded by deep trenches, one of which originally ran across the foreground.

Above right: Part of the old battlefield of Serre.

Below right: A photograph taken from the wall of Serre Road Military Cemetery No. 2., once the site of a major German strong-point. The tall tree in the middle distance is situated near the entrance to Serre Road Cemetery No.1 and Serre itself is behind the trees in the far distance on the right. This whole area was the scene of much slaughter on 1st July 1916.

The cross in the right foreground was erected to the memory of Lieut. Val Braithwaite, 1st Bn. P.A. Somerset Light Infantry, who fell near this spot. The inscription also reads "God buried him and no man knoweth his sepulchre". Beyond, and left of the road, is Serre-Hebuterne French National Cemetery, which contains the graves of 817 French soldiers.

Imperial War Museum

We saw it; we saw men hanging on the wire, some screaming "Shoot me, do me in". The longer they hung on the wire the more they attracted the bullets. It was terrible.

Sydney Booth

7

Above left: Another important part of the old Serre battlefield, just north of Serre Road Cemetery No. 1, and once full of shell-holes and debris of war. Here the British front ran along the face of four copses, named by our troops as Matthew, Mark, Luke and John, parts of which can be seen on the left. Behind those trees is what is now the Sheffield Memorial Park, where old trenches are in abundance. Queen's Military Cemetery is in the lower centre and Serre is about 200-300 yards outside the right hand edge of the photograph.

This picture was taken from Serre Road Military Cemetery No. 3, on 1st July 1973.

Below left: A single cross by the old British front line position in Luke Copse. This simple memorial perpetuates the memory of Private Bull, 12th Volunteers, who was killed on this spot. His remains were found here on 13th April 1928, and transferred to Serre Road Military Cemetery No. 2.

Below: Rare sniper shield discovered on the battlefield by John Giles.

I was in a communication trench, head and shoulders exposed, looking at the whole panorama. Suddenly I heard a crack and a young chap next to me fell dead — shot through the heart by a sniper.

Sydney Booth

The president, Mr. Frank Hartley, aged 78, is seen leading the contingent through the cemetery. Behind him is the honorary treasurer, Mr. Sydney Booth (76); he died in November 1973. The Standard Bearer is Mr. John Pemberton (76). Other Pals present were Mr. Frank Burn, Chairman of the Association (76), Mr. Tommy Danks (79), (Leeds Pals), Mr. H. Oates (74) and Ex-Lieut. G. H. Taylor, M.C., M.M. (79).

BRADFORD PALS COMRADESHIP ASSOCIATION

16th, 18th & 20th Battalions West Yorkshire Regiment

PILGRIMAGE TO FRANCE
29 June to 5 July 1973

On 1st July 1973, a handful of survivors from the Bradford and Leeds Pals Battalions returned to Serre, in company with some other old soldiers, to commemorate the opening of the Somme offensive. At Serre Road Military Cemetery No. 1 they held a memorial service and later went on to Bus-les-Artois, a small village just a few miles to the rear of the old front line, where they were billeted prior to the battle. There, as had been the custom of former years, they enjoyed a slap-up meal in the local estaminet, known to them as the 'Corner Cafe'.

As each year passes the survivors become fewer; one member of the group died on the return journey to England.

Former Bradford Pal, Lieutenant G. H. Taylor (who won his M.C. at Moyenneville in 1918) photographed in front of his one-time billet at Bus-les-Artois. He was stationed there for five months prior to the Somme offensive and went from there to the trenches at Serre at about 8 p.m. on the 30th June 1916. During a discussion he said "Next morning we went over the top and by 7.45 a.m. most of the brigade had been wiped out. The Leeds battalion and the two Bradford battalions were machine-gunned to blazes".

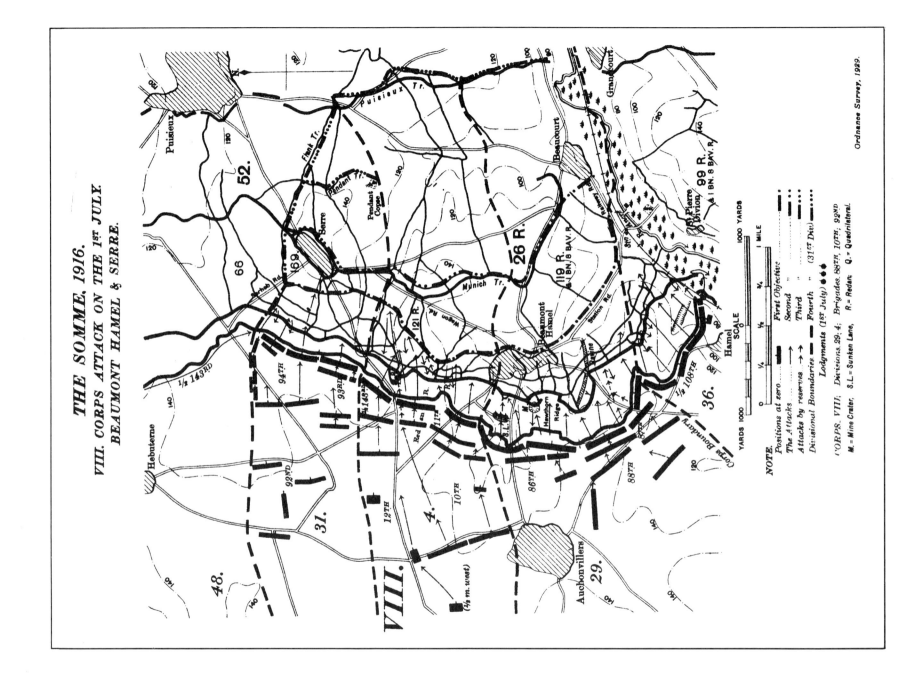

THE SOMME, 1916.

VIII. CORPS ATTACK ON THE 1ST JULY.
BEAUMONT HAMEL & SERRE.

NOTE.

Positions at zero............ First Objective......
The Attacks .... →   Second ....
Attacks by reserves →   Third ....
Divisional Boundaries ─ ─ ─   Fourth " (31ST Div.)
                                 Lodgments (1ST July) ◆◆◆

CORPS. VIII; Divisions. 29, 4; Brigades. 88TH, 10TH, 92ND
M.= Mine Crater, S.L= Sunken Lane,   R.= Redan;   Q.= Quadrilateral.

SCALE

YARDS 1000   0   1000 YARDS

0   ¼   ½   ¾   1 MILE

Ordnance Survey, 1929.

10

FOURTH ARMY: VIII CORPS front continued
29th Division. (Maj.-Gen. H. de B. de Lisle)
(Regular Division)

BEAUMONT HAMEL

The main German defences were located on the hills surrounding the village; one of these, known as the Hawthorn Redoubt, overlooked the Beaumont Hamel — Auchonvillers road. It was the blowing of the mine consisting of 40,000 lbs of ammonal under the redoubt ten minutes before zero hour that finally alerted the enemy to the imminence of the attack. The controversial decision to explode it at that time arose from a disagreement between the corps commander, who wanted it to go up four hours before zero, and the Inspector of Mines who insisted on zero hour itself. General Haig, called upon to arbitrate, decided on 7.20 a.m. a compromise that was the main cause of the heavy casualties. The British guns had to lift their barrage ten minutes early in order to allow our troops to capture and hold the crater, prior to the main assault. In the event, the attack on the crater by the 2nd Royal Fusiliers was unsuccessful.

Bayonet brace — British **SMLE** bayonet top and German **S 98/05** pattern below.

Imperial War Museum

Above: 'OVER THE TOP', a still from the official film, 'The Somme'.

Somehow we get over the wire, our clothes tearing and the barbs scratching and pulling at our bodies and equipment, and we run slap-bang into another gun just behind. Germans jump up and come at us. For a moment there is a flurry of figures, half-seen, hazy faces loom in front of me. I push forward my rifle and let go, working the bolt automatically, and then, as I empty my magazine, slash forward with my bayonet. I glimpse O'Donnell flailing about with clubbed rifle, I hear the short, sharp bark of the subaltern's pistol and suddenly trip over the gun and fall headlong over a struggling and kicking German, who tries to make a grab at me. Oh, my God, as I go down I hear the stutter of another gun close by, and a rushing, whizzing sound of bullets, and then some more spluttering crashes and Rodwell's high cry: "That's for you, you bastards!"

Giles Eyre

11

Left: THROUGH ENEMY EYES. This photograph shows the quite fantastic field of fire afforded to the German machine-gunners and riflemen from the position of the former Hawthorn Redoubt. The British front line went across the valley on the extreme left towards the steep bank, with 'saps' along its base. The main trench system emerged in the fields towards the top centre and proceeded in a north-easterly direction towards the right hand crown of the hill which was known as the Redan Ridge, a notorious area of mining activity. On the right, close to a Scottish memorial cross, is a sunken lane which was used by our troops as a jumping-off trench.

Right: The area to the right of the sunken lane opposite the old Hawthorn Redoubt. In the centre of what was then No Man's Land, and just below another steep bank, is Beaumont Hamel Military Cemetery. The German front line ran down-hill from the redoubt and formed a salient where the bushes jut out from the upper right-hand edge of the picture; after that it went up to the clump of trees on the brow of the hill which marks the location of the Redan Ridge craters.

Imperial War Museum

Also within the area of VIII Corps and near Beaumont Hamel was another major strongpoint consisting of a naturally formed crevasse known as 'Y Ravine'. This was a deep, powerfully fortified position just behind the enemy front line, crammed with machine-guns and barbed wire. These guns caused havoc to the 1st Newfoundland Regiment which, at about 9.15 a.m. had been ordered forward as reinforcements.

Due to the British front line being full of wounded, the Newfoundlanders had to start their move from the support line. They had to cover more than 500 yards to reach the enemy trenches; and within a short space of time 684 members of the battalion, out of a total of 752, became casualties, including 26 officers. Yet the handful of survivors still managed to raise a cheer upon returning to the British lines. The 1st Essex also suffered severely here.

Only one other battalion (10th West Yorks) exceeded that frightful toll that day.

VIII Corps suffered the worst casualty rate of all the British forces engaged on 1st July and achieved nothing. More than 13,000 men were killed, wounded or missing and it took three days to clear the wounded from No Man's Land — even with the help of the Germans who agreed to a temporary truce for that purpose.

Beaumont Hamel was not captured until November 1916 when it fell to the 51st (Highland) Division to whom a memorial was erected in what is now known as Newfoundland Park. (See also pages 115-117).

Above left: **A HELPING HAND.** A wounded man being brought in under fire after the assault at Beaumont Hamel.

Below left: **THE OPEN ROAD.** Beaumont Hamel is beyond the bend in the road. The mine crater is up the hill on the right.

NEWFOUNDLAND MEMORIAL PARK

After the Armistice of 1918 the Newfoundland Government purchased a large tract of ground at Beaumont Hamel; the trenches were preserved, and although they are now grass-covered and mostly no more than shallow ditches, it is not difficult to visualise the task that faced the 1st Newfoundland Regiment.

For a long time the original barbed wire fences were also retained, but these have now gone; the many iron picket bars, however, still in place, give an indication of the thickness of the defences.

The huge bronze caribou stands on a mound of granite on which are recorded the names of 820 men from Newfoundland who gave their lives on land or sea and whose graves are unknown.

Below right: View from the old Newfoundland lines towards the German defences. Beaumont Hamel lies in the distance beyond the trees, and, to the left, on the actual site of the German front line, is a memorial to the 51st (Highland) Division. The notorious 'Y Ravine' runs from left to right just beyond the memorial. Also in that area is what is known as Hunters' Cemetery where men of the 51st Division were buried in a huge shell hole.

Below left: An old trench within the lines from which the Newfoundlanders attacked. Note the huge trench mortar bomb in the foreground and the iron screw picket above.

Above: No Man's Land from the German front line. The Caribou Memorial is near the centre, just in front of the distant trees.

THE BIG DUG-OUT AT BEAUMONT HAMEL. (Extract from Battalion History). It consisted of a shaft, two hundred yards long, penetrating the hillside, with galleries — each with over fifty steps — communicating with the enemy front line. These galleries also connected with tunnels which ran underneath the trenches and were fitted up with wire bunks for the men to sleep on. Electric light was supplied by dynamos driven by oil engines under the entrance of the dug-out. There were sleep bunks for over three hundred men, and although one or two of the entrances had been blocked by shell-fire, the whole construction was in beautiful order. At the end of the long entrance galleries, there were officers quarters fitted with tables and chairs and supplied with looking glasses. Just outside the officers' dug-out was a large church bell, three feet in height and weighing half-a-ton. The clapper was connected by a rope which led up to the sentry in the front line trench, so that, in the event of an attack, warning could be given to the entire dug-out.

W. J. Bradley

THE GERMAN LINES, NEWFOUNDLAND PARK

Bottom: The western end of 'Y Ravine'. This deep, Y-shaped natural cleft, about 500 yards long and, in parts, as much as 40 feet deep, and once full of enemy soldiers, was a major obstacle to any attacking force. Tunnels were driven into the face to link up with the front line and machine-gun positions. Massive shelters were also dug out to protect large numbers of troops from shell-fire.

German 7.92mm Gew 98 rifle recovered by John Giles. Note that the bolt is half open, the rifleman obviously having been shot, in the act of reloading.

Imperial War Museum

Above: The Redan Ridge mine craters which cover an area of about 300 yards by 100 yards, and are still quite easily recognisable. The picture shows why this piece of ground was so bitterly contested by both sides, for it overlooked a considerable area of the battlefield.

Beaumont Hamel is on the extreme left and over the other side of the valley (on the right) is the position of the Hawthorn Redoubt crater. Above and beyond that are the trees of the Newfoundland Memorial Park.

BEAUCOURT HAMEL

Above right: Aerial view of the enemy trenches at Beaucourt Hamel. The station is on the right and Station Road leads off to the left towards Beaumont Hamel.

Apart from being one of the areas where the assault of 1st July broke down after fierce fighting, it was here that the final phase of the Somme offensive ground to a standstill, in appalling conditions, in November 1916.

Below right: A large shell photographed a few yards from Beaucourt Station, July 1973. At the time two ladies were talking, quite unconcerned, just a couple of feet away.

Above: Ruins of Beaucourt Hamel Station (which served Beaumont Hamel) as it was when eventually captured.

BUCKINGHAM PALACE.

I join with my grateful people
in sending you this memorial
of a brave life given for others
in the Great War.

George R.I.

Below left: The station, clean and spruce, in July 1971.

Imperial War Museum

THE ANCRE AT HAMEL: AFTERWARDS

Where tongues were loud and hearts were light
    I heard the Ancre flow;
Waking oft at the mid of night
    I heard the Ancre flow.
I heard it crying, that sad rill,
    Below the painful ridge,
By the burnt unraftered mill
    And the relic of a bridge.

And could this sighing river seem
    To call me far away,
And its pale word dismiss as dream
    The voices of to-day?
The voices in the bright room chilled
    And that mourned on alone,
The silence of the full moon filled
    With that brook's troubling tone.

The struggling Ancre had no part
    In these new hours of mine,
And yet its stream ran through my heart;
    I heard it grieve and pine,
As if its rainy tortured blood
    Had swirled into my own,
When by its battered bank I stood
    And shared its wounded moan.

                                    Edmund Blunden

Above left: 'I heard the Ancre flow . . . ' The Mill Road bridge over the Ancre in 1916, with soldiers collecting water in former petrol cans.

Below left: The River Ancre, which flowed between the opposing lines, passing beneath the present-day bridge; a tributary of the Somme, hardly more than a stream which at some points widens out to become marshlands. From the other side of the bridge can be seen the nearby remains of concrete foundations, once the site of the mill. The hamlet of St. Pierre-Divion lies just beyond the trees. It was heavily fortified and attempts to capture it by men of the 36th (Ulster) Division were beaten back. It eventually fell on 13th November 1916, by which time this area was a sea of mud and desolation.

Above left: View towards, and across, the Ancre (marked by the trees in the centre) with, in the far right distance, Beaumont Hamel in the folds of the hills. The approximate course of the German front line was from the foreground, across the Ancre and then up the hill to the left of the light-coloured field. This picture was taken from the top of the Ulster Memorial.

Below left: THE ULSTER MEMORIAL, THIEPVAL. This memorial, on the former site of the German front line, is an exact replica of Helen's Tower at Clandeboye, near Belfast, and was erected to commemorate the outstanding bravery of the men of the 36th (Ulster) Division during their attack on the Schwaben Redoubt on 1st July 1916, the original anniversary date of the Battle of the Boyne. Over 2,000 men of that division died in this area, and many more than that figure were wounded in 14 hours of severe fighting.

British Mills Bomb and unlocking tool, used for altering delay of fuse.

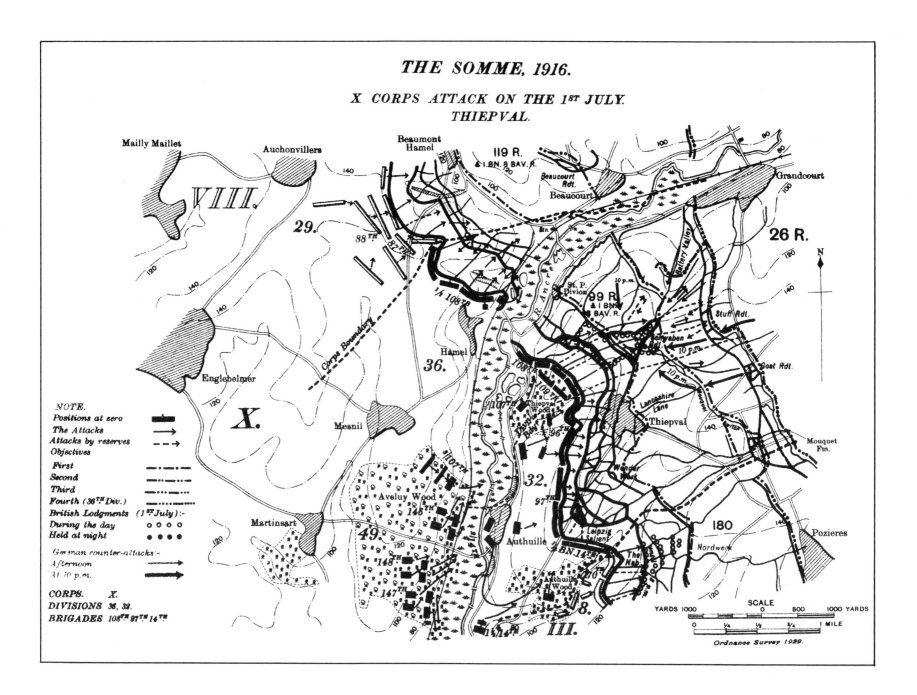

THE SOMME, 1916.

X CORPS ATTACK ON THE 1ST JULY.
THIEPVAL.

NOTE.
Positions at zero
The Attacks
Attacks by reserves
Objectives
First
Second
Third
Fourth (36TH Div.)
British Lodgments (1ST July):-
During the day   o o o o
Held at night   • • • •

German counter-attacks:-
Afternoon
At 10 p.m.

CORPS.   X.
DIVISIONS 36, 32.
BRIGADES 108TH 97TH 14TH

Mailly Maillet
Auchonvillers
Beaumont Hamel
119 R.
& 1 BN. 8 BAV. R.
Grandcourt
VIII.
29.
Beaucourt Rdt.
Beaucourt
26 R.
88TH
82TH
Battery Valley
1/4 108TH
St. P. Division
99 R.
& 1 BN.
BAV. R.
10 p.m.
Stuff Rdt.
Corps Boundary
Hamel
36.
Schwaben Rdt.
10 p.m.
Goat Rdt.
Englebelmer
10 p.m.
Mesnil
X.
108TH
109TH
1/107TH
Thiepval Wood
Thiepval
Mouquet Fm.
Danube Trench
96TH
Lancashire Lane
Wonder Work
Aveluy Wood
146TH
32.
97TH
180
Martinsart
49.
Leipzig Salient
Authuille
148TH
BN. 14TH
Nordwerk
Pozieres
147TH
Authuille Wood
The Nab
8.
1/4 14TH
III.

SCALE
YARDS 1000   0   500   1000 YARDS
0   1/4   1/2   3/4   1 MILE

Ordnance Survey 1929.

20

Above: THE THIEPVAL RIDGE TODAY. This picture was taken from the Ulster Tower, with, on the extreme right, the Connaught Military Cemetery and, beyond that, Thiepval Wood.

Across the foreground once charged cheering men of the 36th (Ulster) Division, under a hail of shells combined with heavy enfilade machine-gun fire from what was left of Thiepval village (upper left) and, in particular, the pulverised ruins of Thiepval Chateau, where now is situated the huge Thiepval Memorial. This memorial (centre right) was designed by Sir Edwin Lutyens, and is the largest of those specifically dedicated to the missing on the Western Front.

It has been said that on the first day of July 1916 Thiepval was masked by a wall of corpses, and that only bullet-proof men could have taken it. Any thought of this being an exaggeration should be dispelled by a visit to the area which gives some understanding of the immense task confronting X Corps at that time.

The ridge — excluding the redoubt — eventually fell into British hands in September 1916, nearly three months after the first assault. It was lost again during the German spring offensive of 1918 but finally fell to our troops, (who on that occasion met with little opposition), in the following August.

Where the trees taper down on the far right of the Thiepval Memorial, is the site of the former Leipzig Salient, in which a positive lodgement was made on 1st July.

THIEPVAL

The front of X Corps stretched from just beyond the Ancre down to a point opposite Authuille Wood, north of Ovillers. The small village of Thiepval was situated in the centre on a hill that dominated much of the surrounding area, including the British lines. It was one of the really great bastions of the German defences on the Somme. These included the Schwaben Redoubt on the northern flank and the Leipzig Redoubt in the south. The village and the redoubts were major strongholds with very deep dugouts, concreted cellars, communication tunnels and masses of barbed wire, behind which were sited numerous machine-guns with splendid fields of fire.

The task of breaking this very hard nut fell to the 36th and 32nd divisions, with the 49th Division in reserve, and the capture of the complete spur and the plateau behind (on which was another redoubt called Stuff Redoubt) was the objective of the day.

Initially the tremendous impetus of the Ulstermens' assault swept them over the Schwaben defences and beyond to the German second line overlooking Grandcourt. The way was almost open for a breakthrough but then tragically they ran into a British barrage and had to fall back. Fierce fighting followed in and around the Schwaben Redoubt as other supporting battalions tried to work their way forward over No Man's Land under extremely heavy shell and machine-gun fire from the village and the ruins of the chateau which were still in enemy hands.

In the 32nd Division's area, six companies had attacked in waves towards Thiepval village but not a man got as far as the German wire after the enemy machine-guns opened up on them, and orders were issued by the commanding officers of the 15th Lancashire Fusiliers and the 16th Northumberland Fusiliers, whose units had been so badly hit, for their remaining troops to stop any further attempts to advance.

Although probably right at the time — particularly in view of the shocking losses and the unexpectedly heavy enemy fire power — this move proved to be disastrous for the 36th Division as it meant that they had no support on their right flank. On their left, too, the attack ground to a halt so that they then found themselves isolated in a salient within the enemy lines. By the time night fell all their hard won gains had been lost, apart from a small section of German trench which they held on to and subsequently handed over to relieving troops.

A little further south other elements of the 32nd Division had been more successful, and a footing had been secured in the Leipzig Salient where bitter fighting continued all day. Constantly the Germans tried to eject the attackers from the redoubt but although pressed hard and eventually being forced to give some ground, these New Army men fought back fiercely and refused to let go of their toe-hold.

This grip on the German line at this point was to be used to advantage in the next phase of the main battle.

Imperial War Museum

Above: THE THIEPVAL BATTLEGROUND. The mound on the skyline is all that remains of Thiepval Chateau. Note the soldier, apparently dead — the only human touch in a dead landscape.

Over 9,000 casualties were caused to X Corps on 1st July, of which more than half were in the Ulster Division. It was a terrible price to pay for what finally turned out to be mainly a defeat; but to its eternal credit, this division from Northern Ireland fought one of the most outstanding actions of the day and certainly deserved better than the fate that befell it.

Above: THE SCHWABEN REDOUBT, THIEPVAL. View from Connaught Military Cemetery with — on the crest — the Ulster Memorial on the left, and Mill Road Cemetery on the right.

Most of the ground shown here was No Man's Land and was covered with dead, dying and wounded men who had taken part in the brilliant action by the 36th(Ulster) Division — one of the few successes of that fateful opening day of the Somme battles. The redoubt was not captured until 14th October 1916 following onslaughts by the 18th and 39th Divisions.

Above: THE LEIPZIG SALIENT. This former chalkpit south of Thiepval was converted into a powerful defence position by the Germans; but in spite of this it was mostly overrun by men of the 32nd Division.

While looking around here in July 1973 the author found several bullets and a human bone where the bank of the chalkpit had given way.

Above right: The grave of Sgt J. Turnbull VC, 17th Bn Highland Light Infantry, who was posthumously awarded the Victoria Cross for most conspicuous bravery and devotion to duty during the bitter fighting in the Leipzig Salient. He held his post almost single-handed against constant counter-attacks, and never wavered. He was killed later in the day while bombing a counter-attack from the parados of his trench. He is buried in the Lonsdale Military Cemetery, near the position of the old salient.

Below right: View across the Ancre towards Thiepval and the Leipzig Salient from near Aveluy Wood on the Albert — Hamel road. This photograph once again emphasises the immense advantage held by the enemy in his defences on high ground.

24

Photo: Commonwealth War Graves Commission

BLIGHTY VALLEY MILITARY CEMETERY

Above: Photograph taken at the end of the war and showing the graves of many men who did not return to 'Blighty'.

Blighty Valley lies south of the location of Leipzig Salient. It became a principal route to the forward trenches after the early July attacks, and constantly received the attention of German gunners. At one time a light railway ran the length of the valley.

Mash Valley, together with Ovillers and, beyond that, La Boisselle, is over the ridge on the right of the picture.

Below left: The same view today. Cornfields and trees have taken over slopes previously bare and scarred by shell holes.

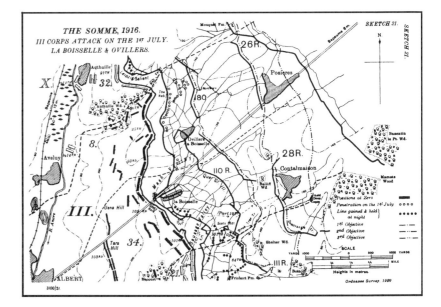

Below: Aerial view of the Ovillers/La Boisselle battlefield area. Becourt village lies in the foreground surrounded by trees, with the trenches, craters and ruins of La Boisselle to the north-west of the wood. (The large white bean-shaped patch is probably the site of Lochnagar crater). Ovillers is on the extreme left-centre of the picture, on the other side of the Albert-Bapaume road which stretches in a north-easterly direction towards Pozières. The latter village is located at the bottom of the line shown on the photograph.

Imperial War Museum

26

FOURTH ARMY: III CORPS (Lieut.-Gen. Sir William Pulteney)
8th Division (Maj.-Gen. H. Hudson) — Regular Division
34th Division (Maj.-Gen. E. C. Ingouville Williams) — New Army Division
19th (Western) Division (Maj.-Gen. G. T. M. Bridges) — New Army Division

OVILLERS-la-BOISSELLE AND LA BOISSELLE

Like so many German-held front line villages, Ovillers and its close neighbour La Boisselle were situated on spurs with excellent observation over the British lines. Both were heavily fortified and were able to give each other supporting cross-fire.

Between these major strong points lay what was known as 'Mash Valley', and on the right of La Boisselle (facing the enemy) was another re-entrant called 'Sausage Valley' by the troops. Some say that this name originated from a German captive balloon stationed at the far end of the valley; others that it was derived from the contours of the ground. Whatever the reason, it was natural for its counterpart to be given the name of 'Mash'.

Bordering La Boisselle, and, in effect, dividing the two valleys, was the very straight former Roman road leading from Albert to Bapaume by way of Pozières (about two miles behind the German line and the original first day objective of III Corps). The position of the road also marked the approximate centre of the Fourth Army front.

At La Boisselle the British and German trenches were not more than about fifty yards apart, and the devastated ground at this point was known as 'The Glory Hole'. It was an area of many overlapping mine craters where bitter hand to hand fighting had taken place continuously when that part of the line had been held by the French. To these craters were added, at 7.28 a.m. on the morning of the assault, two more very large ones on either side of the main Bapaume road.

Dealing with Ovillers first; this village was attacked on the 1st July by the 8th Division but due to the clever siting of the enemy trenches the units on the right flank had to advance more than seven hundred yards up Mash Valley and across ground that was completely devoid of any form of cover.

Imperial War Museum

Above: Battle of Albert. View of the battlefield from the top of Usna Hill and overlooking La Boisselle with, in the far left distance, Ovillers. The British soldiers are on the main Albert-Bapaume road which peters out into a wilderness of ruins and trenches at the bottom of the hill. On the left of the road can be seen the huge mound of chalk thrown up from the 'Y Sap' mine explosion on 1st July. The German main trench followed the course of the road alongside La Boisselle for several hundred yards and then went across Mash Valley at an angle towards Ovillers.

During the attack on La Boisselle the Tyneside Irish had to advance over the open ground shown here towards the German trenches and were wiped out by machine-gun fire. (See page 33).

On the other side of the road the hill was called 'Tara Hill' and a main British trench running at right angles to the road had the name of the Tara-Usna Line. It was from there that the Tynesiders set out full of hope which was shortly to be shattered.

27

We came to the bottom of the valley into a new country. It was a desert of broken chalk-ditches, holes, craters, mounds and ridges, dry and overgrown with weeds, and all interlaced with rusty strands of wire . . . It began to dawn on me that the head of the column must be in La Boisselle, that this was our objective.

There was not a house, nor even a ruined wall left standing and the very line of trees that flanked the road had been blown out of existence. The only landmark was a high rim of white chalk, fifty yards in diameter, like the crater of a volcano, into which the road vanished.

C. E. Carrington (Charles Edmunds).

Above: Photograph taken on 3rd July 1916 from just behind the British front line with, in the centre, the smaller of the two huge mines blown on the 1st. In front of the British trench ran the La-Boisselle-Authuille road. The skeletons of trees behind the crater indicate the former line of the Albert-Bapaume road (along which was located the German front line) and also the utterly destroyed village of La Boisselle. To the right is the area of overlapping mine craters and on the extreme right is that portion of the line known as 'The Glory Hole'. Shells are seen bursting in the distance.

Right: View towards La Boisselle taken from the same position in 1974. The mine crater, which was still there in 1973, has been filled in and the ground cultivated. A new house has been erected near the edge of the old crater.

We are now scrambling over what must have been the British front-line trenches, a maze of humps and hillocks, half-filled-in ditches, mounds of faded and burst sand-bags, barbed wire clumps sticking out here and there, shell-holes, smashed trench-boards and a litter of rusty tins, pieces of equipment, broken rifles and goodness knows what else. We strike out into what was once No Man's Land, a welter of confused destruction and shell-holes.

Here all the casualties have not been gathered in yet, and horrible looking bundles in khaki, once men, still lie in shell-holes.

We pass one close in a shell-hole by the cart track. Lying on his back, his steel helmet half concealing his blackened features. Clothing all awry, legs drawn up. Must have been hit somewhere in the stomach. A storm of fat buzzing flies hover over this poor wreckage of humanity. We hurry by, averting our faces.

Giles Eyre

Above: A photograph taken in 1974 from close to the former position of the British front line at the lower end of Mash Valley. In the distance, on the left, are the church and some of the houses of Ovillers. On the right the line of trees indicate the route of the Albert-Bapaume road. Pozières is beyond the horizon.

The German front line ran along the steep bank on the right and then crossed the valley at an angle of about forty-five degrees, approximately 700 yards away.

On 1st July 1916 this was indeed a valley of death, for men of the 8th Division who attacked along it in the hope of capturing Ovillers came under intense machine-gun fire from both that village and La Boisselle which lies outside the right hand boundary of the picture.

Left: The smaller of the two great mines in 1973 before it was filled in, with, beyond the far lip of the crater, the church spire and village of Ovillers. The depth and the steep sides of the crater clearly indicate the enormous force behind the explosion; unfortunately it did only minor damage to the enemy defences, and was of no real help in the overall assault.

29

Imperial War Museum

. . . As we moved forward a sniper fired almost from behind us. I felt the bullet crack in my ear and Corporal Matthews, who was walking beside me, preoccupied and intent, fell dead in the twinkling of an eye. I was looking straight at him as the bullet struck him and was profoundly affected by the remembrance of his face, though at the time I hardly thought of it. He was alive and then he was dead, and there was nothing human left in him. He fell with a neat round hole in his forehead and the back of his head blown out.

C. E. Carrington (Charles Edmunds)

Above: A photograph taken in September 1916 from close to the Albert-Bapaume road at La Boisselle, showing a couple of British soldiers taking it easy on what was earlier the main German trench that ran from La Boisselle to Ovillers, the ruins of which can be seen in the distance. This was part of the trench system that proved to be a major obstacle to men of the 34th and 8th Divisions on 1st July.

Right: The tranquil countryside of Mash Valley, looking towards Ovillers from the Albert-Bapaume road, on 1st July 1971. (A house has since been built in the centre of the valley, by the roadside.) The line of the former German trench shown in the picture above can still be seen at the near end of the valley as depicted by the bushy area. The original trench followed the course of the minor road and then came out in a large bulge towards the top.

Imperial War Museum

Above: Looking down 'Mash Valley' from Ovillers Military Cemetery, towards La Boisselle and the former position of the British lines. In the distance are Tara and Usna Hills, divided by the Albert-Bapaume road, over which the Tyneside Irish advanced to their doom.

The cemetery contains over 3,300 graves, one of which is that of Captain John C. Lauder, son of the late Sir Harry Lauder of Music Hall fame. Two thirds of the overall graves are of unidentified soldiers.

Above right: 1916. Communication trench running through the ruined village of Ovillers. The jagged piles of bricks were all that was left of the church. The attack on the village on 1st July was repulsed with heavy losses, and it was not until 16th July, after bitter fighting, that the remnants of the German garrison surrendered. They had fought with exceptional bravery and only two officers and 126 men remained unwounded. This small group surrendered mainly to bombers of the 11th Lancashire Fusiliers. Other units of the 25th Division and the 32nd Division had also battled furiously in and around the village before it finally came into our hands.

Below right: 1971. The main street of Ovillers. It is much like other villages of the Somme area with a somewhat straggly line of houses and a church.

Presently I saw a likely trench cutting across the valley, and having no news of Bickersteth, decided to risk it. I went on in front of the party to pick the way. There was mud in the bottom, though the sides were white chalk, and a few corpses at that repulsive stage when the skin turns slimy black, so I followed the example of the men, climbing out and followed the parapet.

It was then, turning back, that I knew what the novelists mean by a "stricken field". The western and southern slopes of the village had been comparatively little shelled; that is, a little grass had still room to grow between the shell-holes. The village was guarded by tangle after tangle of rusty barbed wire in irregular lines. Among the wire lay rows of khaki figures, as they had fallen to the machine-guns on the crest, thick as the sleepers in the Green Park on a summer Sunday evening. The simile leapt to my mind at once of flies on a fly paper. I did not know then that twice in the fortnight before our flank attack, had a division been hurled at that wire encircled hill, and twice had it withered away before the hidden machine-guns. The flies were buzzing obscenely over the damp earth; morbid scarlet poppies grew scantily along the white chalk mounds; the air was tainted with rank explosives and the sickly stench of corruption.

C. E. Carrington (Charles Edmunds)

Above: A very large unexploded shell, excavated during 1973 trench digging operations at the eastern end of Ovillers.

Left: Looking towards Ovillers from the Albert-Bapaume road, July 1974. It was here (where traces of trenches are still visible) that C. E. Carrington (Charles Edmunds) — who, in his famous book 'A Subaltern's War', vividly describes the fighting in this area — led his men to take part in the final phase of the battle for the village.

Royal Engineers cap badge (left) and Royal Army Ordnance Corps badge unearthed on the Somme battlefield.

Intense machine-gun fire from both villages flayed the leading waves as they attempted to advance and men fell in droves all over the valley. Then came further carnage as the German guns put down a hurricane of high explosives. Frightful casualties were incurred by the 8th Division to the extent that the division later had to be taken out of the line and placed in reserve. One battalion — the 8th Yorks and Lancs — suffered almost ninety per cent losses and other units came very close to that total. Almost 150 men from the 2nd Middlesex got as close as the Pozières road but they then disappeared and were not heard of again. Only 50 men from that battalion answered roll call that day.

The 34th Division, which was on the right of the 8th Division, had the task of storming La Boisselle and, at the far end of Sausage Valley, the village of Contalmaison. Firstly they were to capture the enemy trenches on either side of the Albert-Bapaume highway at La Boisselle and then the village itself, for which purpose the divisional commander had allocated two brigades. The third brigade of the division (Tyneside Irish) which was some way to the rear in a position known as the Tara-Usna Line, was then to take advantage of any gap made and push forward. If the German defences collapsed from this pressure the situation was to be exploited by the 19th (Western) Division and also Gough's cavalry which was being held in readiness for that purpose.

Therefore, at 7.30 a.m., all three brigades of the 34th Division rose from their trenches and, as happened everywhere else, the German machine-guns opened up on the advancing troops with devastating effect.

From the Tara-Usna line the 3,000 men of the Tyneside Irish Brigade set off across completely open ground towards the British front line and — so they expected — a way through the enemy positions. They had almost a mile to travel, and as they passed down the slopes of Tara and Usna Hills with their bayonets glinting in the sunshine, they became a perfect target for the incredulous Germans. Streams of lead cut swathes in the ranks; yet still the survivors struggled onwards. Practically all of the 2nd and 3rd Battalions were wiped out before they got to the British front line; and very many of the 1st and 4th Battalions as well.

Imperial War Museum

Above: Troops of the 34th Division advancing to the attack on La Boisselle.

Then — and perhaps this is the greatest tragedy of all — the remnants of the two right hand battalions continued on into No Man's Land in conformance with their original orders and there the vicious machine-gun fire and shell-fire destroyed more of the men until very few were left. Well inside the German lines this pitifully small group joined up with a similar handful from the two leading brigades, which had also been decimated, and headed for Contalmaison. However, the village was heavily defended by a strong trench system and other fortifications and much more than the incredible bravery of a few men would have been needed to take it.

33

Below: The entrance to La Boisselle village, 1974, from the bottom of Usna Hill. The straight road leads to Bapaume and the right fork to Contalmaison. The big mine crater was just beyond the house on the left and on this side of it is the civilian cemetery, through which part of our line passed prior to the offensive. In the distance, on the extreme left, is the village of Ovillers.

On the right of the photograph — and this side of the trees — is a stone seat which is a memorial to commemorate the attack by the 34th Division.

The 34th Division lost more heavily than any of the 14 divisions that attacked during the course of the day on 1st July 1916, with the Tyneside Scottish and Tyneside Irish being particularly hard hit. About 80 per cent of men from the leading 12 battalions of the division became casualties — most of them within ten minutes of the start of the assault — and only a small part of La Boisselle was captured that day.

As the 8th Division lost around 5,000 men, with no gains, the nett result for the corps had been almost total failure at a tremendously heavy cost.

Base of fired gas shell — denoted by the hollow, thin walled casing.

We crossed the ground, slowly picking our way through the half-obliterated trench-lines up hill and down dale; past the bare, tortured ground of what had been La Boisselle. Scarce a brick remained of it, and the site could only be traced by a signpost.

Giles Eyre

I left the cemetery and wandered on to the recently captured craters of Ovillers, originally made by months of mining and counter-mining by the enemy and the French. This place, like a huge ravine, was linked by subterranean tunnels which subsequently joined on to a maze of trenches. It had cost hundreds of lives to take, and the enemy may well have thought the place impregnable. From the edge of one of these craters I looked down the sides, covered in rusty barbed wire, where clusters of corpses grilled in the hot sun, khaki and grey uniforms indiscriminately mixed. To shelter from the glare rising off the chalky, tortured ground, I scrambled down into this hecatomb, where, like the dead staring at the roof of blue sky, I felt separated from this world.

Paul Maze

Below: Recent picture of some of the smaller mine craters at La Boisselle, the scene of ferocious underground fighting when the sector was held by the French.

Right: Two badly wounded Germans being assisted to the rear by British Tommies.

Imperial War Museum

German water bottle — the bullet that left its mark on this relic was undoubtedly fatal to its owner.

35

We scrambled on past all the pitiful litter and on to that gash of chalky hummocks and dirty bags running across our front that had been the German front trench.

Here the havoc was unimaginable and stood revealed in all its ghastly details under the rays of the bright sun. A strange, mephitic, undescribable smell hung about here like a tangible pall. Bodies were numerous, twisted in all the attitudes of death. Quite a lot of ours — Lincolns, Scots, Yorks, mostly in shell-holes before the trench. This itself was practically flattened out, bags all down and destroyed, but here and there the opening of dug-outs stood unharmed.

Bloated, grey-clad figures littered the whole place. Some crouching against the sides, some lying stark and still, sightless eyes staring up at the blue vault of heaven. One dead German on a stretcher with bandages all over him, by a dug-out entrance.

Giles Eyre

Above left: Entrance to a dug-out in the former German front line, La Boisselle, July 1916. Note the masses of barbed wire on the parapet.

Below left: Part of the old German front line system at La Boisselle, July 1973, close to 'The Glory Hole' and the craters.

Below: LOCHNAGAR CRATER. The interior of the larger of the two main craters at La Boisselle, the result of the explosion of 60,000lbs of ammonal. It is over 300 feet across and about 90 feet deep — note the cows. The Somme craters, unlike their counterparts in the Ypres Salient — which rapidly became miniature lakes — remained completely dry.

Above: Two Mills grenades and a rifle grenade awaiting collection by the authorities at the roadside at La Boisselle, in July 1971.

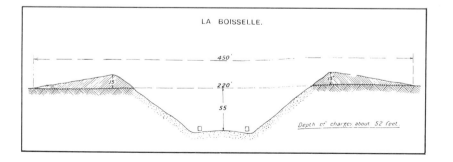

LA BOISSELLE.

450'

220'

55

Depth of charges about 52 feet

Below left: British troops around field kitchens in 'Sausage Valley' in May 1917.

Below right: 1973. Sausage Valley, looking towards Contalmaison. In the foreground can be seen signs of old trenches and shell holes. Close by is the Lochnagar crater, which is wired off. Now the property of Richard Dunning of London, who purchased it to ensure its preservation.

Right: A German observation balloon. These were well protected by anti-aircraft weapons, and although to some British airmen 'balloon busting' was considered to be a sport, it was also an extremely hazardous occupation. Rockets attached to the wings of the aircraft were one of the weapons employed.

Imperial War Museum

Imperial War Museum

FOURTH ARMY: XV CORPS (Lieut.-Gen. H. S. Horne)
21st Division (Maj.-Gen. D. G. M. Campbell) New Army Division
17th (Northern) Division (Maj.-Gen. T. D. Pilcher) New Army Division
(50th Brigade)

THE FRICOURT SALIENT

Fricourt lay just within the German lines and formed a pronounced salient which was the cornerstone of the enemy defence system on the Somme front. It was, of course, similar to all the German held villages in the battle zone having been converted into a veritable fortress that incorporated a maze of trenches, strong points and very deep dug-outs.

For this reason, it was decided not to make a frontal attack on the village, but to outflank it and Fricourt Wood (to the rear of the village and also heavily defended), with a view to isolating the position for later capture.

The 21st Divison would go in to the north of Fricourt with, on their right — and covering Fricourt village — one brigade (50th) of the 17th (Northern) Division. The remaining brigades of 17th Division were in reserve at the rear.

In spite of a very heavy barrage by artillery and Stokes mortars combined with gas and several large mine explosions, German machine-guns still survived, and created carnage among the troops attempting the left flanking movement and virtually annihilated two companies of the 10th Battalion West Yorks (50th Brigade). Their casualties amounted to 710, including 22 officers — the highest battalion loss for any single day during the war.

Imperial War Museum

Above right: Fricourt and the German defence system under artillery fire prior to the assault of 1st July 1916.

Below right: Photograph taken from the location of the old German front line near the Tambour mine craters. The enemy here had complete advantage in height and observation, plus a superb field of fire. Part of Becourt Wood (once just behind our lines) can be seen on the right, and the chimney stack in the centre — with trees running diagonally to its right — marks the position of the main road to Albert, along which much of our transport (and, of course, troops) had to come. Movement was only possible during the hours of darkness.

Above left: The interior of a German dug-out at Fricourt, July 1916. This very well-built and wood-lined shelter (probably belonging to a senior German officer) emphasises the efforts made by the enemy to make life in the trenches as comfortable as circumstances permitted. To the British, such a dug-out would have been real luxury.

Looking across to Fricourt; trench mortars bursting in the cemetery; dull white smoke slowly floats away over grey-green grass with buttercups and saffron weeds. Fricourt Wood (full of German batteries). North, up the hill, white seams and heapings of trenches dug in chalk. Sky full of lark song.

Siegfried Sassoon

Right: A converted Mk.VII naval gun, one of the weapons employed in battering the Fricourt defences. It fired a 6-inch shell.

Other troops on the left of Fricourt belonging to the 63rd and 64th Brigades of the 21st Division also suffered severe casualties through machine-gun fire from Fricourt; on the right too a company of the 7th Green Howards, which carried out an unscheduled attack at 7.45 a.m., was wiped out within a few yards of its jumping off position.

As a result of misplaced optimism on the overall situation on the flanks a direct attack against Fricourt was ordered for 2.30 p.m. by General Horne, Due mainly to faulty heavy artillery ammunition the wire was only partly cut and the three remaining companies of 7th Green Howards, together with follow-up companies of 7th East Yorkshires — all of 50th Brigade — came under murderous machine-gun and rifle fire. As at Thiepval and elsewhere, the Germans even stood on the parapet to shoot at the attackers. Only very few reached Fricourt, and most of them were cut off and destroyed. A handful survived by hiding in cellars.

Units of the 22nd Brigade (7th Division) also met with a bloody repulse on the right of the fortress.

Nevertheless, gains were made on either side of the village, and during the night of 1st/2nd July the surviving Germans withdrew.

Imperial War Museum

There were about forty casualties on the left (from machine-gun in Fricourt). Through my glasses I could see one man moving his left arm up and down as he lay on his side; his face was a crimson patch. Others lay still in the sunlight while the swarm of figures disappeared over the hill. Fricourt was a cloud of pinkish smoke. Lively machine-gun fire on the far side of the hill. At 2.50 no one to be seen in No Man's Land except the casualties (about half-way across).

Siegfried Sassoon

Above: Ruins in Fricourt, July 1916, with British troops and wagons (or artillery limbers) on the left, amidst smashed trenches and barbed wire.

Right: THE FORMER BATTLEFIELD OF FRICOURT. A photograph taken on 1st July 1971 of one of the major battlefields of the 1916 fighting on the Somme. The cornfield shown here was a sea of red poppies on this warm, sunny day, and high above a lark sang over what once was the scene of bloody conflict and tragedy.

On these pleasant slopes, which long ago were swept with machine-gun fire and high explosives, died many men of the West Yorks, East Yorks and Green Howards. On the right centre is Fricourt No. 3 New Military Cemetery, in which is the grave of sixteen year old Private A. Barker. Beyond the Cross of Sacrifice are hummocks of earth which mark the location of the Tambour mines, blown on the morning of 1st July 1916. Fricourt Church is on the left centre and part of the strongly defended Fricourt Wood is on the extreme left.

Fricourt was abandoned by the enemy during the night of 1st/2nd July as it had been outflanked by the capture of Mametz on the right wing.

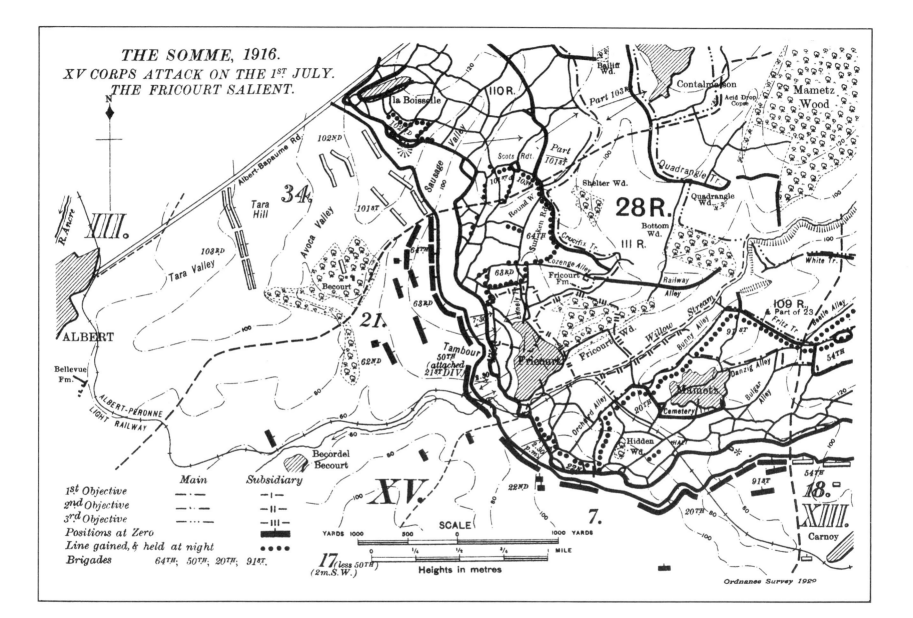

THE SOMME, 1916.
XV CORPS ATTACK ON THE 1ST JULY.
THE FRICOURT SALIENT.

1st Objective
2nd Objective
3rd Objective
Positions at Zero
Line gained, & held at night
Brigades   64TH; 50TH; 20TH; 91ST.

Main   Subsidiary

SCALE
YARDS 1000   500   0   1000 YARDS
0   ¼   ½   ¾   1 MILE
Heights in metres

Ordnance Survey 1920

42

The village was a ruin and is now a dust heap. A gunner (Forward Obervation Officer) has just been along here with a German helmet in his hand. Said Fricourt is full of dead; he saw one officer lying across a smashed machine-gun with his head bashed in — "a fine looking chap," he said, with some emotion, which rather surprised me.

Siegfried Sassoon

Above left: The road out of Fricourt, July 1916, with German prisoners being marched out to 'the cage'. The ruins of the village can just be seen in the centre.

Below left: The same place, July 1971. The woman with the pram is almost at the same spot as the leading horseman in the photograph above.

Above: Part of the German Military Cemetery — a rare thing on the Somme battlefield — at Fricourt, containing approximately 5,000 graves.

43

MAMETZ

Mametz, to the right of Fricourt, was situated on the southern arm of the L-shaped front and close to the Albert-Peronne road. Inevitably it was heavily fortified with excellent observation from well sited enemy trenches and strong points. Part of these powerful defence positions had been incorporated into the civilian cemetery to the south west of the village.

In December of 1914 a severe action had been fought at Mametz and a certain amount of mining activity had later taken place during the French offensive-defensive operations.

The capture of the village was the prime objective of the 7th Division, a Regular formation that had experienced hard fighting in Flanders during the early part of the war. Several New Army battalions were now included in its ranks and these men would be going into action for the first time.

Two of the battalions of the 7th Division that were to be very much involved, were the 8th and 9th Devons of 20th Brigade. An officer of the 9th Battalion, Captain D. L. Martin, was convinced, through his knowledge of the ground, that there was an enemy machine gun position built into a wayside shrine at the cemetery which could easily wipe out attacking troops. Whilst on leave in England he made a plasticine model of the battleground, which confirmed him in his beliefs, and he informed his brother officers when he returned to his unit. He was proved right when he went over the top with his battalion and the machine gun at the shrine opened up on them causing many casualties. Among the dead was Captain Martin.

In spite of the heavy losses inflicted by this weapon and others, the advance continued and within a comparatively short time the outskirts of Mametz had been reached.

Running through Mametz was a major trench called Dantzig Alley where enemy resistence became tougher. In addition counter attacks were hurled against our troops by the Germans; but with the aid of reinforcements and a fierce artillery barrage our men continued to smash their way forward.

By the middle of the afternoon practically all of Mametz was in British hands.

At the end of the day the 21st and 7th Divisions of XV Corps had suffered over 7,500 casualties. To this number must be added another 1,100 from 50th Brigade of 17th Division, of the same corps, thus making an overall total of more than 8,500.

To offset these heavy losses, Mametz had been captured and Fricourt, which had been outflanked on both sides, was to be given up by the enemy overnight.

In comparison to other parts of the front this was considered to be a major success.

Above: **THE GORDON CEMETERY.** This small, isolated military cemetery, just below Mametz, is beside the Albert-Péronne road and contains the remains of 93 men and six subalterns of the 2nd Battalion, Gordon Highlanders, of the 7th Division, who were killed almost immediately after they went over the top at the beginning of the battle, and were buried together in their jumping-off trench. The German front line was only a few hundred yards away.

MAMETZ.

Above left: View towards Mametz from close to the position of the former British front line. Almost in the exact centre of the photograph (beyond the second field) is the civilian cemetery, on a high bank, which, in 1916, was a powerful enemy stronghold. To the rear of the spot where this picture was taken is a small wood known as Mansell Copse, in which was sited the British front line.

170 men of the Devonshire Regiment lie buried in the old front line trench in Mansell Copse, which later became the Devonshire Cemetery (seen below). An Officer of the 9th Devons, who died at that time and is buried there, was William Noel Hodgeson, a war poet and contemporary of Rupert Brooke.

Below left: Mansell Copse from the civilian cemetery.

Above: Battle of Albert. British troops attacking German trenches on 1st July 1916 at Mametz. The white mounds indicate trenches from which chalk has been excavated; the smoke cloud is from a bursting shrapnel shell.

As we went up the lane toward Mametz I felt that I was leaving all my previous war experience behind me. For the first time I was among the debris of an attack. After going a very short distance we made the first of many halts, and I saw, arranged by the roadside, about fifty of the British dead. Many of them were Gordon Highlanders. There were Devons and South Staffordshires among them, but they were beyond regimental rivalry now — their fingers mingled in blood-stained bunches, as though acknowledging the companionship of death. There was much battle gear lying about and some dead horses. There were rags and shreds of clothing, boots riddled and torn, and when we came to the old German front-line, a sour pervasive stench which differed from anything my nostrils had known before.

Siegfried Sassoon

Above left: RAMC ambulances collecting wounded in the ruined village of Mametz, July 1916.

Below left: Mametz main street, 1974.

At 2a.m. we really began to move, passing through Mametz and along a communication trench. There were some badly mangled bodies about. Although I'd been with the Battalion nearly eight months, these were the first newly dead Germans I had seen. It gave me a bit of a shock when I saw, in the glimmer of daybreak, a dumpy, baggy-trousered man lying half sideways with one elbow up as if defending his lolling head; the face was grey and waxen, with a stiff little moustache; he looked like a ghastly doll, grotesque and undignified. Beside him was a scorched and mutilated figure whose contorted attitude revealed bristly cheeks, a grinning blood-smeared mouth and clenched teeth. These dead were unlike our own; perhaps it was the strange uniform, perhaps their look of butchered hostility.

Siegfried Sassoon

47

We set off up the hill, passing the grey and red ruins of Mametz village on our left as we walked up towards Pommiers Redoubt. The guns were firing, and an occasional shell-burst crashed through the air with a venomous answer. Transport was crawling about in the distance, small groups of men were moving, dark against the white gashes of the chalk. Scattered equipment lying about underfoot, tangles of wire, small dumps of forgotten stores, all left behind in the advance. Other things were left behind in the advance, part of the purchase price of this downland, grim disfigured corpses rotting in the sun, so horrible in their discolour that it called for an act of faith to believe that these were once men, young men, sent to this degradation by their fellow men.

Llewelyn Wyn Griffith

Photo by courtesy of Col. G. B. Jarrett, Ret'd.

Above right: **DANZIG ALLEY MILITARY CEMETERY.** Danzig Alley was the name of a major enemy trench that ran through the centre of Mametz village from the apex of the civilian cemetery and in the general direction of Montauban which, like the former position of Pommiers Redoubt, lies outside the right hand limit of this photograph.

The cemetery contains over 2,000 graves of which more than 500 are of unknown soldiers. It overlooks what was known as Death Valley and the notorious Mametz Wood which can be seen to the right of, and beyond, the Cross of Sacrifice. The spire of Contalmaison church is faintly visible in the far distance on the extreme left and Pozières lies on the distant ridge left of centre. Near the Cross of Sacrifice is a memorial to the 14th (S) Bn. Royal Welsh Fusiliers, 38th (Welsh) Division.

Left: There is nothing to show whether this hand belonged to a British soldier or a German, but it is possible that its former owner is one of those named on the Thiepval Memorial to the Missing.

Imperial War Museum

FOURTH ARMY: XIII CORPS. (Lieut.-Gen. W. N. Congreve. V.C.)
18th (Eastern) Division (Maj.-Gen. F. I. Maxse) — New Army Division
30th Division (Maj.-Gen. J. S. M. Shea) — New Army Division

CARNOY and MONTAUBAN

The XIII Corps front was on the extreme right of the British line and ran from just east of Mametz along to the village of Maricourt, junction point of the Anglo-French Armies.

A short distance to the rear of the British trenches was the small village of Carnoy, on a road leading to Montauban which was little more than a mile away within the German lines. It was that enemy-held village and the ridge on which it stood that was the final objective of the day for the Corps.

Two other principal features were in the area of the corps, the Carnoy craters and the Pommiers Redoubt. The craters were a series of large holes caused by the explosions of mines in earlier minor engagements and it was here that some bitter hand-to-hand fighting took place at the beginning of the assault. Pommiers Redoubt was a major strongpoint on the ridge, below which was what was known as Casino Point. Here a large mine had been prepared but this was inadvertently blown late, after our men had gone over the top, and the resultant debris caused numerous casualties to the attackers.

Above: Aerial photograph showing clouds of gas rising from the trenches N. E. of Carnoy.

The gas appears to be drifting towards the enemy trenches from the British front line astride the Carnoy — Montauban road. The ruins of these two villages are bottom right and top left respectively. Bernafay Wood can be identified at the very top of the picture, on the left. Pommiers Redoubt would be outside the north western limits of the landscape. At the time when this photograph was taken — probably at the end of June 1916 — gas was in regular use by both sides, having been introduced on the Western Front by the Germans in April 1915, at the time of 'Second Ypres', when it almost enabled them to obtain the long sought breakthrough. The Allies retaliated shortly afterwards, and it became a constant battlefield hazard to all the combatant troops during that war.

It was a cold but clear night when we moved off at intervals by companies for an old dug-out line near Carnoy, some three miles march away. At 10 p.m. we found ourselves on the high ground on the northern outskirts of this shell-scarred village. Our "billets" for the night were to be the network of abandoned and shell-shattered trenches which were the Huns' front line up to the first day of this great Somme offensive, 1st July, '16.

F. C. Hitchcock

49

One of the units that was involved in the battle and which belonged to the 18th Division, was the 8th East Surreys. Before the assault Captain W. P. Nevill, a company commander, purchased several footballs for his platoons with the object of 'kick-off time' being 7.30 a.m. on the 1st July and No Man's Land the pitch. His men did jump off with each platoon kicking a ball towards the enemy but Captain Nevill did not, unfortunately, live to see the end of the match, and he is buried in Carnoy British Military Cemetery.

Soon after zero hour, all the early objectives of the 18th Division were taken; and on their right the 30th Division also advanced successfully. Due to considerable help from French heavy guns, Montauban had been practically levelled to the ground, the German trenches — including numerous deep dug-outs — were battered out of existence, the barbed wire had been well cut, and the defenders were badly demoralised by the overwhelming weight of the barrage. Additionally, several tunnels had been dug across No Man's Land and at the appointed time, small charges were set off at the exits, enabling our troops to debouch into, or close to, the enemy defences.

Here and there, as the battle progressed, single surviving machine-guns gave considerable trouble, but they were dealt with by the artillery which, on this corps front, was handled far better, from a tactical angle, than anywhere else along the line. It included, for the first time ever, the innovation of the creeping barrage. Another factor of importance was that 'mopping up' operations took place as the men advanced — unlike many other areas, where the Germans came up from dug-outs behind our troops, who were then attacked from the rear.

By midday all the objectives of XIII Corps had been taken, in spite of a stiffening of resistance at various places. Montauban

Imperial War Museum

Above right: The old Carnoy craters where fierce hand-to-hand fighting took place on the first day.

Below right: An 18-pounder gun team in action, Carnoy Valley, July 1916. The pile of shell cases on the right indicates that they have been having a busy time.

fell about mid-morning, after some fighting amidst the ruins, and Pommiers Redoubt came into our hands after bitter close-quarter engagements.

Without doubt the best results of the day occurred on this right flank of the line, where the French, too, met with considerable success and attained all their objectives. In front of XIII Corps, which now overlooked Mametz Wood and Bernafay Wood (with Trones Wood nearby) the situation appeared to be ripe for exploitation. A patrol entering Bernafay Wood found it deserted, as was the open ground nearby. Everything pointed to a further successful advance being feasible, but when General Congreve asked Rawlinson's permission, it was refused.

We were to pay dearly for this error of judgement in the coming weeks. Even the Germans, who had expected us to advance further, were surprised, and very soon reorganised their forces. By the time orders had been issued for a resumption of the attack, they were again manning strong defences on the southern flank, and the woods were crammed with their machine-guns and troops.

In the fighting for Montauban and the ridge XIII Corps lost over 6000 men in killed, wounded and missing. Although this was a terrible toll for the amount of ground taken, the operation was a success compared to other parts of the line.

Enemy losses were also heavy with, on the 30th Division's front, 3,000 out of 3,500 Germans becoming casualties — many of them from the crushing artillery barrage directed on the village and defences by British and French guns. The French 'heavies' were especially useful in this area.

Above right: Montauban, once totally destroyed, now calm and peaceful.

Below right: AREA OF LOST OPPORTUNITY. A 1974 view from close to the site of Montauban brickworks, captured on the first day of the offensive by men of the 30th Division. Part of Bernafay Wood is on the left and Trones Wood is centre right.

Although undefended by the enemy, Bernafay Wood was not occupied until July 3rd.

CASUALTIES OF 1st JULY

According to the Official History, total casualties of all ranks on 1st July 1916 amounted to 57,470, of which 19,240 were killed or died of wounds, 35,493 were wounded, 2,152 were missing, and 585 were taken prisoner. Practically all were infantrymen.

This was the greatest loss ever suffered by the British Army in a single day of its history, with many battalions being virtually annihilated and some divisions losing a major proportion of their effective fighting strength.

Most of the casualties occurred in No Man's Land, before the German trenches had even been reached.

As I stepped over one of the Germans an impulse made me lift him up from the miserable ditch. Propped up against the bank, his blonde face was undisfigured, except by the mud which I wiped from his eyes and mouth with my coat sleeve. He'd evidently been killed while digging, for his tunic was knotted about his shoulders. He didn't look to be more than eighteen. Hoisting him a little higher, I thought what a gentle face he had, and remembered that this was the first time I'd ever touched one of our enemies with my hands. Perhaps I had some dim sense of the futility which had put an end to this good-looking youth. Anyhow I hadn't expected the Battle of the Somme to be quite like this . . .

Siegfried Sassoon

PART 2

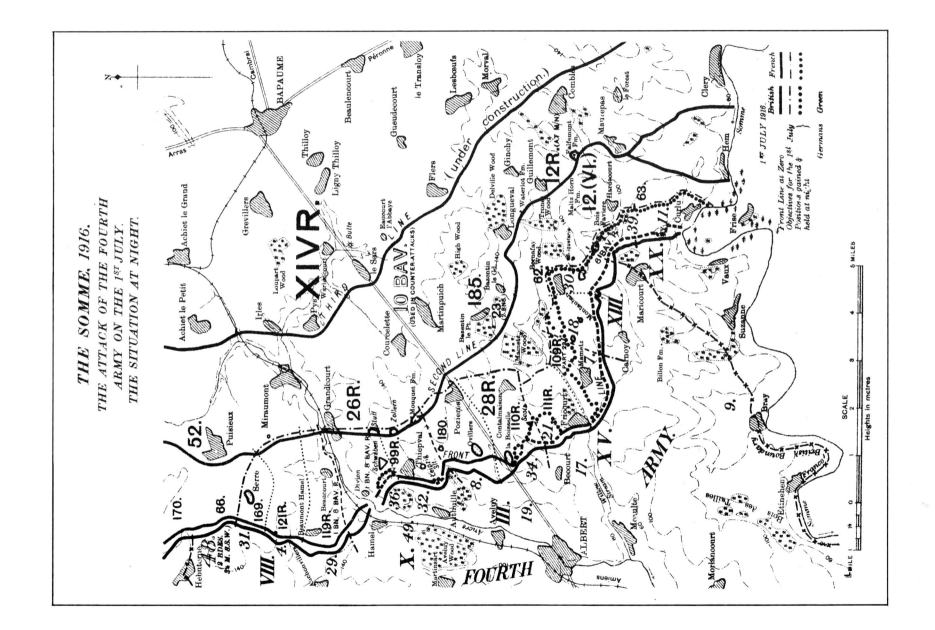

THE SOMME, 1916.

THE ATTACK OF THE FOURTH ARMY ON THE 1ST JULY.

THE SITUATION AT NIGHT.

THE FOLLOWING DAYS

In view of the breakdown in the assault of July 1st on the western arm of the L-shaped front, Sir Douglas Haig changed his original plans which had aimed at the capture of the Thiepval plateau. Instead the new objective was the exploitation of the success gained by the seizure of Mametz and Montauban, coupled with the abandonment of Fricourt by the enemy.

Meanwhile, it was necessary, due to the terrible losses of the first day, to carry out some reorganisation of our forces; and on the evening of 1st July, General Gough was directed to take command of the shattered X and XIII Corps. At the opening of the offensive the General's Reserve Army had grown to three cavalry divisions and two infantry divisions but as the hoped-for breakthrough did not occur, this Army was accordingly unable to function in its planned role. In fact, the two infantry divisions (19th and 49th) were thrown into the general struggle under the auspices of the Fourth Army.

By the 4th July the Reserve Army (the title of which was changed on 30th October 1916 to Fifth Army) consisted of nine divisions. Six of these divisions had already been severely mauled while part of the Fourth Army.

On the right flank preparations were put in hand for the second phase of the main assault. July 14th was chosen as the date of the attack, which was to be directed against the German second line between Bazentin le Grand and Longueval, on the Pozières-Ginchy ridge. However, prior to the opening of this next phase, it was necessary for our troops to secure Mametz Wood, Contalmaison and Trones Wood, and orders to that effect were issued on July 8th.

On 4th July heavy rain fell along the front and continued intermittently over the next few weeks, and operations were hampered by the mud, which was hated for its clinging, chalky consistency. Matters were made worse by the fact that our troops still had to fight their way uphill, for the German positions were mostly sited on high ground, whence the enemy could use his deadly machine-guns to advantage.

Above: LEADERS CONFER. General Sir Douglas Haig with General Sir Henry Rawlinson at Fourth Army Headquarters, Querrieu, July 1916.

Below: OWNER AT HOME. Comte Jacques d'Alcantara de Querrieu standing on the steps of his chateau, July 1973. Under his right arm the Count is holding a visitors book filled with the signatures of many famous people, including royalty and military and civilian leaders of the 1914-1918 war.

By determination, courage and sheer stubborness, our troops overcame all these disadvantages — and those that followed later — but not before the casualty lists had grown at a horrific rate. The Germans, in turn, fought tenaciously to hold back the slowly advancing Allies, and their casualty lists, too, reflected the dour struggle.

Over on the left, severe fighting continued in front of, and around, Ovillers, with constant British attacks being bloodily repulsed by machine-gun fire from the rapidly dwindling number of Germans clinging to the ruins of the village. As mentioned elsewhere, what was left of Ovillers did not fall to our troops until 16th July, after the remaining handful of Germans were almost completely surrounded.

La Boisselle, on the other hand, came into our possession after four days of ferocious fighting. Thus the carnage continued.

We had reached the high ground at Pommiers Redoubt, and standing in a trench, scanning the wood with our glasses, it seemed as thick as a virgin forest. There was no sign of life in it, no one could say whether it concealed ten thousand men or ten machine-guns. Its edges were clean cut as far as the eye could see, and the ground between us and the wood was bare of any cover. Our men were assembled in the trenches above a dip in the ground, and from these they were to advance, descend into the hollow, and cross the bare slope in the teeth of the machine-gunners in the Wood. On their right, as they advanced across the bullet-swept zone, they would be exposed to enfilade fire, for the direction of their advance was nearly parallel to the German trenches towards Bazentin, and it would be folly to suppose that the German machine-guns were not sited to sweep that slope leading to the Wood.

Llewelyn Wyn Griffith

Right: **View towards Mametz Wood from the Mametz-Montauban road, from about the former position of the Pommiers Redoubt. The Pozières Ridge is beyond the wood, and practically in the centre of the horizon is the Thiepval Memorial. Just to the right of the memorial, and nearer to the wood, is Contalmaison Church.**

MAMETZ WOOD

Across the rising ground between Mametz Wood and Contalmaison ran an enemy trench called the Kaisergraben, the lower part of which was captured by troops of the 52nd Brigade (17th Division) on the night of 4th/5th July and subsequently renamed Quadrangle Trench. To the right of this strong position, next to Mametz Wood, was Wood Trench, mostly still held by the Germans. Mametz Wood itself was a tangled mass of almost impenetrable undergrowth and fallen trees laced with barbed wire. Along the southern edge were numerous German machine-gun emplacements. They covered sloping ground over which our troops would have to attack from the direction of what was known officially as Caterpillar Valley, and by many of our soldiers as Death Valley. The latter name was the more realistic of the two.

An attack against the wood was mounted by the 38th (Welsh) Division on the night of 8th/9th July, but this failed to achieve any satisfactory result; and a fresh attack by the Division was arranged for 4.15 a.m. on the 10th. Meanwhile the wood — and particularly the southern part — underwent a heavy bombardment by British guns.

The 38th Division made its new assault and some success was met with on the flank. In the centre heavy losses occurred due to the open nature of the ground but in spite of this the southern edge was subsequently occupied and the advance continued, with much difficulty, within the wood. On the far right, at Flat Iron Copse (where there is now a British cemetery), strong opposition was encountered and this caused much trouble.

Eventually the centre of the wood was reached and, under heavy fire, the Welsh troops fought on until they were fifty yards from the northern edge. On their left the 17th Division was also heavily engaged.

During the night the Germans bombarded the wood unmercifully and the tired men suffered numerous false alarms.

On the 12th July the exhausted Welshmen were relieved and went into reserve with the division having lost nearly 4000 of all ranks. Seven battalion commanders were amongst that total.

An indescribable smell rises up; the air is thick with it. Bits of equipment everywhere, broken-down barricades, barbed wire catching at our feet, now and again dead bodies half concealed by rubbish and foliage can be glimpsed. And over all the din of our bombardment, the occasional crash of a Boche shell in the thickets, the machine-guns tap-tapping somewhere in Mametz Wood.

We come again to the open, with the bare slope rising in front of us. Mametz Wood is just beyond. Here a maze of trenches, heaped with khaki and field-grey figures, debris of all kinds.

Giles Eye

Above: **DEATH VALLEY.** The bare, open ground leading to Mametz Wood on the left, with, in the foreground, what was probably a British trench. It was here that the 38th (Welsh) Division lost heavily through machine-gun fire coming from the wood.

At the far end of the valley is Flat Iron Copse Military Cemetery and, beyond that, the former position of the German second line on Bazentin Ridge.

The remainder of the wood was cleared by units of the 62nd Brigade which, in turn, lost close to 1000 officers and men from the effects of enemy shell-fire and gas, until relieved on the night of the 15th/16th July.

German rifle pouch and shovel cover found on the Somme battlefield — an indication of the relics that still abound today.

Above right: British artillerymen inspecting a captured German gun in Death Valley. In the rear can be seen the very steep bank down which our infantry had to clamber in order to get to the wood. Note the cross in the bank at the left.

Below right: This recent picture of the same bank was taken from a former German trench just inside the edge of the wood. The probable British trench (page 55) is situated this side of the car.

My first acquaintance with the stubborn nature of the undergrowth came when I attempted to leave the main ride to escape a heavy shelling. I could not push a way through it and had to return to the ride. Years of neglect had turned the Wood into a formidable barrier, a mile deep. Heavy shelling of the Southern end had beaten down some of the young growth, but it had also thrown trees and large branches into a barricade. Equipment, ammunition, rolls of barbed wire, tins of food, gas-helmets and rifles were lying about everywhere. There were more corpses than men, but there were worse sights than corpses. Limbs and mutilated trunks, here and there a detached head, forming splashes of red against green leaves, and, as in advertisement of the horror of our way of life and death, and of our crucifixion of youth, one tree held in its branches a leg, with its torn flesh hanging down over a spray of leaf.

Llewelyn Wyn Griffith

Above: The interior of Mametz Wood, showing a captured German gun. From the shape of the gun-carriage it is possible that this is one of the old French 'overbank' fortress guns from Mauberge, two batteries of which were used by the enemy in the wood, until they were taken by our troops.

Left: Tractors bringing up 8-inch howitzers, Death Valley, near Mametz, July 1916. The men are taking cover from shells bursting on the far side of the road which was an important route to the forward battle zone following the capture of Mametz Wood.

CONTALMAISON

This village, defended by a well-wired enemy trench system, was situated between the German first and second lines. It commanded the rising open ground to the west of Mametz Wood and although included in the objectives of 1st July, was not taken until ten days later.

Heavy showers occurred on the 7th July as preliminary attacks were mounted by the 17th Division of XV Corps against the forward enemy defences. Mud considerably hampered operations, and machine-gun fire, both from the village and Mametz Wood, caused serious losses to the assaulting troops. The 6th Dorsets were particularly hard hit on this occasion.

On the left the 1st Worcesters of 24th Brigade (23rd Division of III Corps) forced their way into Contalmaison as far as the church but then had to fall back, after a struggle of some hours, when their supplies of bombs and ammunition ran out.

Further attempts to advance were made by the 50th and 51st Brigades of 17th Division but once again heavy machine-gun fire and a fierce artillery barrage forced back the attackers with considerable losses.

On the 9th July, with the weather having improved, units of the 23rd Division pushed their way forward south and west of Contalmaison and the 69th Brigade made preparations for an all-out attack on the village. This was timed for the next day at 4.30 p.m., the aim being for the Green Howards and the West Yorks to join hands in the north-western part of the village.

The 50th and 51st Brigades of 17th Division also endeavoured to fight their way forward by a surprise night attack on the 9th July but once again intense enemy fire broke the attack before the all-important German trench called Quadrangle Support was reached. In spite of its heavy casualties this division gamely took part in further bitter fighting on the 10th July and that same night was relieved by the 21st Division, having lost nearly 4,800 officers and men.

Meanwhile, and as had been the case for some days, Contalmaison was subjected to continuous bombardment by British guns. At the appointed hour, the Green Howards and the West Yorks moved forward and, against further stout resistance from the Germans, joined hands at about 5.30 p.m. By that time the 8th Green Howards had been reduced to 8 officers and 150 men.

An enemy counter attack developed in the late evening but this was driven back with no more attempts being made by the Germans to retrieve the ruins.

On the 11th July the 1st Brigade of General Strickland's 1st Division relieved the 23rd Division which up to that date had incurred losses amounting to almost 3,500 men.

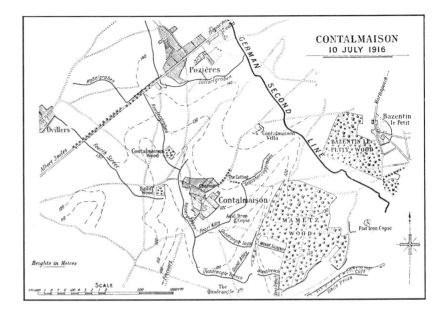

The sound of a heavy bombardment, some distance away to our left, broke in upon the silence and grew to a storm of noise and smoke. Contalmaison was the target, prominent upon a hill until the smoke obscured the hill-top, turning it into a dark cloud hung between a blue sky and brown-pitted earth. Out of this cloud, at intervals of some minutes, an orange sheet of flame made an effort to escape, only to be conquered and smudged out by the all-pervading smoke. It did not seem possible that there could be guns enough in France to create such a fury as this . . .

Llewelyn Wyn Griffith

Below: Contalmaison, bathed in sunlight, from just north of Fricourt, with, in the right distance, the ill-famed Mametz Wood. The powerful Quadrangle and Kaisergraben trenches (see map of Contalmaison opposite) ran roughly through the centre of the picture. Contalmaison was the first-day objective of the 34th Division of III Corps, but the attack broke down at La Boisselle (see page 33). The village fell, after bitter fighting, to troops of the 69th Brigade on the 10th July.

59

Imperial War Museum

Rifle bolt from an early example of the German Gew 98. The damaged runner would seem to indicate that this one exploded in the firer's hands.

Above left: Ruins in Contalmaison; the cross marks the position of the church, September 1916. Below left: Contalmaison rebuilt.

French Infantryman's steel helmet recovered by John Giles.

Above: The entrance to a massive German underground shelter in the northern corner of Bernafay Wood, July 1916, following its capture, on the 3rd, by men of the 9th Division.

In July 1971 the author tried to locate it, without success; the wood had grown up and hidden it.

Above right: British and German wounded, near Bernafay Wood, 19th July 1916. One of the men is wearing a stretcher bearer's armband.

Above: 18th Division memorial, Trones Wood.

Below: July 1971. Ex-Private Charles Williams revisits Trones Wood after 55 years. As a young soldier he was wounded during the fighting for the wood and subsequently had a leg amputated.

TRONES WOOD

At 8 a.m. on the 8th July — an earlier combined French-British attack having been postponed for twenty four hours — men of the 30th Division advanced towards Trones Wood while our Allies also pressed home an attack from their sector. Heavy machine-gun and rifle fire caused serious losses to our troops who were compelled to fall back to Bernafay Wood. Another attack was then mounted and this time the southern end of Trones Wood was entered by the 2nd Wilts with limited casualties. They were reinforced later by 18th Kings and units of the Manchesters.

Early on the morning of the 9th the central and northern parts of the wood were captured by the 17th Manchesters and Maltz Horn Farm, over on the right, was taken by the 2nd Royal Scots Fusiliers. Powerful counter-attacks developed, and there then followed a period of dreadful carnage in the dense, shell-torn undergrowth of Trones Wood.

For the next few days attack followed attack as both sides advanced or fell back. Time and again the wood changed hands in vicious fighting and under most trying conditions, including terrible shell-fire. Everywhere were dead British and Germans, bloodstained equipment and clothing, parts of bodies, ammunition and all the detritus of war. The 2nd Bedfords suffered heavy casualties, as did the 20th Liverpools south of the wood, but the Germans also had serious losses. Flame throwers were brought into use by the enemy in a desperate attempt to clear the British from the wood but heavy fire from our guns broke up that particular attack before it had really got under way.

During the evening of the 12th July the battered 30th Division was relieved by the 18th Division after having lost 90 officers and over 1,800 other ranks. The 18th planned to complete the take-over during the night.

At 7 p.m. that evening the 7th Buffs and 7th Royal West Kents went into the southern part of the wood with 7th Queens and 8th East Surreys in support. The West Kents came under heavy artillery fire and, although again hit hard by small arms fire inside the wood, two companies pushed on so far that they became cut off from the main force.

By now serious concern was being felt at XIII Corps headquarters as it was imperative for the wood to be taken in order to ensure that the main attack on the German second line was not adversely affected. The task of securing the wood, once and for all, was handed over to the 54th Brigade and at 4 a.m. on the morning of the 14th the brigade went forward with the 6th Northants leading the way. Fierce fighting took place but by 9 a.m. the northern edge of the wood had been reached and the whole area cleared of the enemy. The West Kents, who had been isolated, were re-united with their comrades as the surviving Germans fell back towards their second line at Guillemont Station and Waterlot Farm. The 12th Middlesex played a principal role in the final capture of the wood.

Although one more counter-attack was planned by the enemy, this did not materialize, for by then Longueval had been entered, and the strongpoint of Waterlot Farm had also fallen to our troops.

The bloody, shell-shattered stumps of Trones Wood were now firmly in possession of the British. Five major attacks had been hurled against it by our forces and four equally strong counter-attacks had been mounted by the Germans. Once again a few acres of woodland, blasted and burned almost beyond recognition, had become a mass graveyard.

Above right: Photograph, taken from a corner of Trones Wood, of a bombardment near Ginchy, September 1916. The trench in the foreground was possibly an old German communication trench leading towards the enemy second line which is under fire.

Below right: A recent photograph from the same place, where once was a major German strongpoint, and looking towards Ginchy. Waterlot Farm is beyond the trees on the left, close to Delville Wood and Longueval (see map on page 68). Guillemont station was once situated near the farm on the right and Guillemont village is on the extreme right.

At dark we started off again, and all went well until we entered Trones Wood. Suddenly the enemy put down a box barrage all round the wood. Luckily we had good cover in the C.T. which the Battalion had dug some weeks previously, called "Leinster Avenue". A Company had also a carrying party out under Sharp; they were in front, and had decided to halt, so there we were jammed up in the trench. The open was impossible, owing to the fallen trees and thick undergrowth, so we had to lump it, listening to the shells raining down all round, sniffing the smell of a number of decomposing corpses, mostly those of German gunners who had tried to hold the wood in the first few days of the offensive. I sent a message to Sharp, asking him if it was safe to push on, but he sent L/Corpl. Ronan, M.M. (A Company Stretcher-bearers' N.C.O.), to say it was quite impossible owing to the barrage in front. We were just half an hour in that stinking wood. At last we moved on, without a single casualty, to the front line, and returned at 2 a.m. to the Battalion.

F. C. Hitchcock

German Pickelhaube pierced top centre by rifle fire or shell splinters — undoubtedly fatal. The inscription reads 'With God for King and Fatherland'.

THE BREAKING OF THE GERMAN SECOND LINE POSITION
(THE BATTLE OF BAZENTIN RIDGE)

The mid-July attack against a four mile front of the German second line position was timed to start at dawn on the 14th, following an assembly by night of the main assault troops. These were 9th and 3rd Divisions of XIII Corps, who were to advance between Delville Wood and Bazentin le Grand village, and the 7th and 21st Divisions of XV Corps on the left, covering Bazentin le Grand Wood and Bazentin le Petit Wood (just north of Mametz Wood). On the extreme left troops of III Corps were to carry out an auxiliary attack.

At first, Sir Douglas Haig was firmly against the plan, particularly the difficult night-time operation of concentrating unseasoned troops fairly close to the German positions, and his doubts were shared by the French. But General Rawlinson insisted that the scheme was workable, and was backed by his corps and divisional commanders. General Haig finally sanctioned the attack, and preparations continued at full speed.

On 11th July the preparatory bombardment began, but, due to a shortage of heavy howitzer reserves, ammunition for the big guns was rationed. Unlike 1st July, however, a creeping barrage was to precede the advance and was to prove highly successful. Meanwhile three cavalry divisions were ordered to be ready to move, with High Wood and Martinpuich being two of their principal objectives. The seizure of High Wood was considered by General Rawlinson to be of vital importance, and the 2nd Indian Cavalry Division was allotted this task. In the air the Royal Flying Corps reigned supreme, and this permitted the siting of dumps of ammunition and stores well forward in the battle area, and even in the open.

At the last minute the French decided not to attack in their sector, south of Guillemont, with their XX Corps, but to limit their assistance to a heavy supporting artillery barrage. This was an unexpected set-back for the commander of the Fourth Army, General Rawlinson, but he was determined to continue with the second phase of the overall battle.

Although things went well during the early part of the assault — particularly on the left where the Bazentins fell quite quickly — the fighting for the ridge turned into a vicious battle of attrition with tremendous losses being suffered by both sides. Once again, too, the cavalry could not be used for its proper role even though a minor attempt was made to break through the enemy line between High Wood and Delville Wood.

In the latter — known, with good reason, as 'Devil's Wood' — the South Africans were to win immortal fame. Although numerous British units were involved in the bitter fighting for Longueval and Delville Wood — many of them being New Army battalions — the main glory belongs rightly to the South Africans, whose terrible losses adequately reflect the ferocity of the struggle.

A bare valley sloped down from us and rose again to the Huns, who were clinging to a few clumps of tree stumps, bushes and wreckage of parched, sered greenery forming the outlying approaches to Bazentin Wood. Our own trenches sloped down and then bent sharply through the wood, the Bazentin villages and beyond to Trones Wood.

But what a shambles stood revealed to our eyes! Bodies of British and German soldiers formed practically a carpet from our parapet right across the valley and to the very edge of the Boche line. Dead men, shell-holes and bits of arms! In the hollows and patches of dead ground over this eight hundred yards of terrain the slain in all the horrible attitudes of sudden death, were lying in heaps, Briton and Hun intermingled, at peace at last! To see these heaps of poor, mangled and rotting flesh, shapes which a few days previously had been healthy, vigorous men in the prime of life, full of laughter and the zest of youth, with ambitions, strength, vitality, now blackening and breaking up under the blazing heat of the July sun, made one think of the utter futility and pity of it all.

Giles Eyre

Below: **A senior citizen of Bazentin le Petit takes a stroll in the sunshine amidst peaceful surroundings, July 1974.**

Above: **Part of the former powerful German second line trench system near Bazentin le Petit village, 1974.**

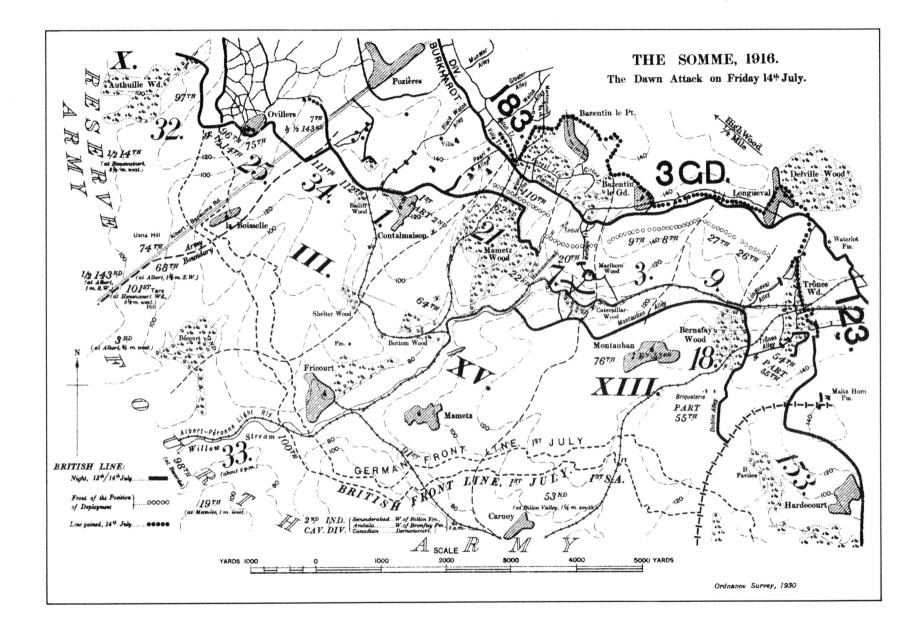

THE SOMME, 1916.
The Dawn Attack on Friday 14th July.

X.

RESERVE ARMY

Authuille Wd.
100TH
97TH
32.

1/2 14TH
(at Beaussincourt,
8½ m. west.)

1/2 143RD
(at Albert,
1m. S.W.)

101ST Tara
(at Henencourt Wd.,
5½ m. west.)
Hill

3RD
(at Albert, ¾ m. west.)

Usna Hill
74TH
68TH

III.

Bécourt

N

Albert–Péronne Light Rly.

Willow Stream
100TH
(at Bécourt)

98TH
(at Bécourt)

33.

19TH
(at Meaulte, 1 m. west.)

2ND IND.
CAV. DIV.
{ Secunderabad...W. of Billon Fm.
Ambala.........W. of Bronfay Fm.
Canadian.......Dernancourt. }

96TH
75TH
½ 14TH

Ovillers
7TH
& ½ 143RD

120
100

la Boisselle
120
100

2.
34.
111TH
112TH

Army Boundary

Shelter Wood

Fm.

Fricourt

Bottom Wood
80

XV.

Mametz

100
120

91ST FRONT LINE, 1ST JULY.
GERMAN
BRITISH FRONT LINE, 1ST JULY. 1ST S.A.

53RD
(at Billon Valley, 1¼ m. south.)

Caruoy
8 a.m.

BURKHARDT DIV.
Munster Alley

Pozières

Gloster Alley
Welsh Alley

183

Bazentin le Pt.

High Wood
¾ Mile

Black Watch Alley
Villa
140

Pearl Alley
1ST
ART 2ND

120
Bailiff Wood

1.
Contalmaison.

62ND

Mametz Wood

22ND

64TH

100

80

Villa T.

Breat T.

Circus
Snout
110TH

Bazentin le Gd.
140

3 GD.

Longueval

Delville Wood

21.

20TH
Hammerhead
Marlboro' Wood

3.
Caterpillar Wood

9TH 140 8TH
27TH
26TH

Waterlot Fm.

Longueval Alley

123.

9.

Trônes Wd.
Guillemont Fm.

54TH
PART 55TH

140

Montauban
76TH

Bernafay Wood

18.

XIII.

Briqueterie
PART 55TH

Dublin Alley

Maltz Horn Fm.

B. Faviere
120

153.

100

Hardecourt

BRITISH LINE:

Night, 13th/14th July. ━━━━

Front of the Position } ○○○○○○
of Deployment

Line gained, 14th July. ●●●●●

YARDS 1000   0   1000   2000   3000   4000   5000 YARDS
SCALE

Ordnance Survey, 1930

66

Delville Wood

THE SOUTH AFRICAN STORY

18th July 1916. Aged 16

At 3,25 a.m. on the morning of 14th July, when the assault on Longueval and Delville Wood began, the South African infantry brigade numbered 121 officers and 3,032 men.

At 6.20 p.m. on the evening of 20th July, when the last units were finally relieved, three officers and 140 men were all that came out of the line. Even when all the remnants of the brigade were eventually reassembled only 29 officers and 751 men were found to have survived.

These figures convey better than any words the intensity of the struggle in which the South African contingent in France fought, first to take and thereafter to retain, one of the most exposed and crucial salients on the Western Front at that time.

The importance of the area lay in the fact that whoever controlled it was possessed of a wedge of high ground with which the formidable German second position might well be prised open. This was realised by the commanders on both sides, Haig and Rawlinson being as eager to seize it as Falkenhayn and Below were determined to retain it.

The assailants' task was an unenviable one. Not only would they have to make their way uphill in the face of seasoned troops in concealed and entrenched positions, but, once established within the salient, they could have their communications interrupted by, and themselves be subjected to, converging fire from three directions.

This hazardous assignment was entrusted to the 9th Division, of which the South African infantry brigade formed part. This division, originally wholly Scottish, belonged to the 'First Hundred Thousand' of Kitchener's volunteer army, and numbered among its component elements units from such illustrious regiments as the Black Watch, the Royal Scots, and the Argyll and Sutherland Highlanders. During the fighting of the preceding year, it had become a name to conjure with, on both sides of the front — not least on account of its exploits at Loos, where for a time it had actually captured the awesome Hohenzollern redoubt and the equally forbidding Fosse 8. The price of glory, however, had been casualties beyond the capacity of the Highlands to replace, and in

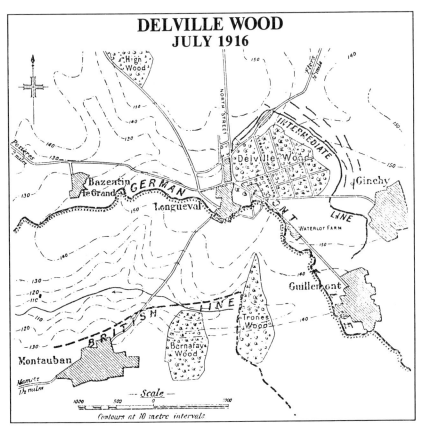

DELVILLE WOOD
JULY 1916

Scale

Contours at 10 metre intervals

Above right: The ruined village of Longueval, September 1916. The men on the left are engaged in road repairs.

Below right: Longueval, on the road to Montauban. It was near this spot that the powerful German second line trench ran.

the end the merging of some units and the disbandment of others had become imperative.

It was as part of this process of re-organisation that the South African contingent, fresh from its experiences in Egypt, had come to be attached to the 9th in April 1916. That this allocation was a compliment to the new arrivals was beyond dispute; but the 'old hands' of the division were at first little disposed to bestow compliments on anyone. 'The inherent clannishness of the Scots,' their historian records, 'revolted at the idea of friends being taken away and of strangers coming in.' The news of the change and of the choice of a replacement was received 'with consternation.' Nonetheless, following the first parade inspection, it was generally agreed that the new recruits were 'very impressive' and 'an exceptionally fine body of men,' and following the first joint exercises, even the most fastidious clansman had been won over to the conviction that the division had been 'greatly honoured in having such a doughty brigade attached to it'.

Since the South Africans had had little experience of trench warfare, save for their brief spells at the front for training and acclimatisation during the quiet months of May and June, and since, following the catastrophe at Loos where the 21st and 24th Divisions lost 8,246 out of 9,600 men in their first engagement (without inflicting a single casualty on the enemy), it had become accepted practice not to place unseasoned troops in the vanguard of attack, the plan of campaign for 14th July required the 26th and 27th Brigades to storm Longueval village and thereafter seize Delville Wood, with the South Africans in reserve for 'mopping-up' operations in both cases. The two positions were considered interconnected, since neither could be held for long without the other.

The attack on Longueval in the early hours of 14th July met with initial success. The front-line garrison was taken completely by surprise, and quickly overwhelmed. Thereafter, however, resistance stiffened. Not for nothing had Falkenhayn issued instructions to his men to yield not an inch: 'Nur uber Leichen darf der Feind seinen Weg vorwarts finden'. (The enemy must not be allowed to advance except over corpses.) Typical of the defen-ders' attitude was the response of a small German detachment to an offer of quarter by a body of Highlanders who had completely surrounded them:

'*I and my men,*' their officer replied, *have orders to defend this position with our lives. German soldiers know how to obey orders. We thank you for your offer, but we die where we stand.*'

And they did. The outcome, in general, was bitter, costly, hand-to-hand and house-to-house fighting, made worse for the attackers by the fact that their preliminary bombardment had not been sufficient to pulverise the village, let alone collapse the network of subterranean shelters and passages that lay beneath it, but had, in many cases, served only to tumble the masonry, so providing the defenders with numberless nooks and crannies within access of the underground communication tunnels from which to harass them undetected.

By the afternoon of the first day, Longueval had still not been taken in its entirety. This had consequences for the advance on Delville Wood, since the seizure of the village was judged an essential prerequisite for any operations against the adjacent territory. Even more important, the heavy losses of the Highlanders in the street fighting necessitated their reinforcement within the village, and their replacement outside it, by the troops of the divisional reserve.

Thus it came about that the South African Infantry Brigade was called upon, first to take, and thereafter to retain, 'at all costs,' the area known as Delville Wood.

The attack, after repeated postponements made necessary by the inconclusiveness of the fighting in the village, eventually got under way at 5 a.m. on 15th July. Progress was slow, though less on account of enemy action — the garrison had been thinned out as a precaution against the expected bombardment of the area — than owing to the nature of the terrain. Delville Wood, an area roughly 154 acres in extent, had been described by one who had known it before the war as a 'thick tangle of trees, chiefly oak and birch, with dense hazel thickets intersected by grassy rides.' The brief preliminary bombardment had served only to heighten the difficulties, by adding shell craters and fallen trees to the previously existing obstacles. In the words of the British Official History, 'even the rides were not easy to recognise, being partly obliterated by craters and debris'. Nor did the men's equipment make things any easier. In addition to the standard kit, 66 pounds in weight, each soldier was burdened with an assortment of other objects ranging from carrier pigeons and tins of fresh water to ammunition boxes and rolls of barbed wire. The day, which had started overcast and cool, soon showed a hot and cloudless countenance. 'I can assure you,' one survivor subsequently recalled, 'every time we trekked the perspiration simply ran off me in rivers.'

By midday, the South Africans had cleared the wood and reached the perimeter in every sector except the north-west corner. Intense shelling then almost immediately began. Since counter-attacks could be expected at any moment, the South Africans were instructed to dig themselves in. This was easier said than done. The chalky soil, matted with roots and tangled with branches, offered resistance to the most resolute spade. Work was further interrupted by rifle and machine-gun fire from the enemy intermediate trenches not seventy yards away, while a succession of counter-attacks at battalion strength put paid to concerted digging for much of the afternoon. The most important result of these frustrations was that the ten machine guns which General Lukin, the officer commanding the Brigade, had planned to hold the perimeter could not in all cases be adequately mounted. This meant that the men in the line could not be dispersed as a precaution against artillery bombardment, but had to be concentrated along the 1,800 yards of the perimeter. For lack of alternative cover, many took refuge in the abandoned German trenches. Those were an uncertain haven, since the enemy artillery knew their exact location. The outcome, as one survivor later described it, was less than reassuring:

'The Germans started shelling us, and they did not half give it to us hot; of course, they knew every inch of the trenches. They started at the one end and finished at the other end, we were like rats in a trap, we could not get one way or the other.'

So anxious was Gen. Sixt von Arnim, the German com-mander on this sector of the front, to recapture the lost salient, that further attacks were ordered for that night. Reinforcements were hurriedly assembled, and, despite protests from battalion commanders that there was insufficient time for adequate preparations, the attacks were set for midnight in the wake of a three-hour artillery bombardment. In the words of the official historian of the 9th Division, 'a hurricane of shells swept Delville Wood.' In all, three determined onslaughts were made, each preceded by artillery fire, and each from a different direction. Although these were repulsed with rifle and machine-gun, the enemy's lachrymatory shells gave the defenders a lot of trouble. Writing to his parents, one survivor has left us this account:

'Before attacking they sent over tear shells, which blind your eyes with tears, tears streaming down your face. The pain is awful. One can hardly breathe, and there is a terrible burning in the nose, throat and lungs. The idea is to interfere with one's shooting, since one cannot see the sights on the rifle in front of one's face. Unfortunately, our tear shell goggles are useless, and only make things more unpleasant, becoming quite opaque with tears so that it is quite impossible to see.'

The next day, 16th July, an attempt was made to take the yet uncaptured north-west corner, and clear it of its irksome garrison. Since the South African and German positions were considered too close together to permit of any artillery preparation, the attack had to be made with the support of trench mortars only. Despite the great gallantry displayed — one participant was to be awarded the Victoria Cross — the enemy machine-guns proved more effective than bayonet borne courage alone; and after incurring heavy losses the effort had to be discontinued.

The following day, 17th July, a further attempt was made — again without artillery support — and again nothing to show for it but casualties. Otherwise, the pattern of events followed a distressingly familiar pattern: shelling, followed by counter attacks, followed by further shelling.

Living conditions, already very bad, deteriorated steadily further. Rain, alternating with a parching heat, was one source of discomfort.

B Company was now allotted a line of sorts, connected shell-holes on the extreme edge of Delville Wood. In this trench we were approximately situated. We experienced difficulty in getting to this line. We all ran the gauntlet from enemy snipers, who were extremely vicious. One by one we ran from shell-crater to shell-crater, bullets whizzing past and slapping the earth beside us. Our dead lay all over the place. I remember in the fold of the ground two men sitting up straight, their mouths wide open, and full of horrible black flies!

F. C. Hitchcock

This crushed mess-tin could doubtless tell a tale of one man's suffering.

Right: Aerial view of Longueval; the long whitish patch is all that was left of the village; the stumps to the right of it, all that was left of Delville Wood.

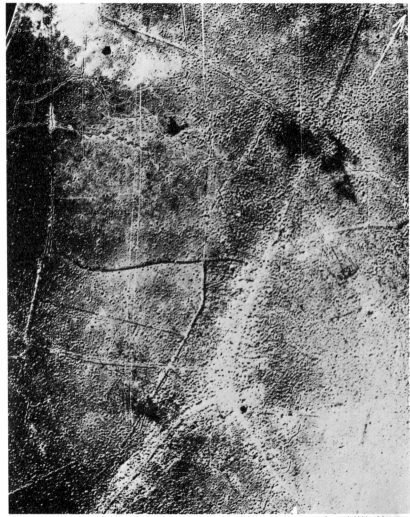

Above left: The old British front line in Delville Wood, July 1917, showing the utter desolation and a few remaining shell-shattered trunks.

Below left: Memorial obelisk in Delville Wood, July 1973. The inscription reads, ''Here in a shallow trench stood the battle headquarters of the South African infantry during the fighting in Delville Wood''.

Below: The 'South African tree' in Delville Wood; it grew from the roots of a shell-blasted stump which nature has now enclosed within the sturdy trunk.

'*From July 4-10,*' one survivor recalled, *officers and men had neither blankets nor greatcoats; it rained at least every other day, and one never got a decent sleep. We were either crouching down in the trenches to get cover from shells, or lying out in the wet grass, until shells dropping close made it advisable to get into the trenches.*'

Fatigue was a yet more serious matter. One survivor, in a letter to his mother, noted simply:

'*Some of our boys were so tired that they stood sound asleep with their rifles at the shoulder.*'

Snipers were a growing hazard for those awake as well as for those asleep. A machine-gunner has left us this account:

'*A sniper crept up and got in a shell hole just in front of us; could barely see his head. From there he watched and pulled down chap after chap of ours, nearly all in the centre of the head.*'

There were also many cases of shell-shock. One soldier noted simply:

'*A fellow with shell shock is just like a frightened child. Trembles violently, weeps, and requires someone to take charge of him.*'

All this, however, paled into insignificance with the bombardment that began at sunset on the evening of 17th July, continued throughout the night, and then, from 8 a.m. on 18th July, suddenly reached and sustained a rapidity of fire rarely equalled elsewhere. From an examination of German regimental histories it is clear that altogether 116 field guns and upwards of seventy medium and heavy guns, not to mention howitzers of every calibre, were used for the bombardment of an area roughly 1,000 by 1,200 yards. For seven and a half hours shells rained on the defenders, often at the rate of 400 to the minute. The earth trembled and shook. The sky became quite dark with the smoke of burning branches and the debris from the explosions. The noise was deafening — the crash of falling trees mingling with the scream of shells and the heavy concussion of high explosive. One survivor has given this account of his reactions and experiences:

'*The terrible awful fear that a concentrated bombardment gives you is indescribable. You hear the shell coming, and cower in the bottom of the trench, and then, say fifty yards away, the trench flies in the air in a blinding flash and an awful noise, and men you know have been utterly blotted out. No piece is ever found, and if it was a 12-inch there is a hole that an ox-wagon could hide in, and this goes on at the rate of thousands of shells an hour on a front of 500 yards.*'

Another wrote to his mother:

'*Our position was so well marked, that they could drop shells right into it; shrapnel, lyddite, high explosive, tear and gas shells. What I prayed for, and I think what we all prayed for, was an instantaneous death. The sufferings of the wounded around us quiet unnerved me. I never for one moment expected to come out alive. And there we sat; no food nor water; nothing could get through; friends dying on every side.*'

To make matters worse, the British counter-battery fire was not always accurate, shells often landing in the South African positions.

The lot of the wounded, and the stretcher bearers who valiantly sought to transport them to the dressing stations, was the worst of all. One of the luckier of the latter who, though wounded, survived, has left us this account of the experiences of the South African Medical Corps:

'*I and three other bearers were despatched for duty with the regiment. We came under a fairly heavy bombardment during the night, one of our party sustaining shell shock, which necessitated his removal to the dressing station. The three of us were kept extremely busy, and were not relieved until we had been carrying patients for 27 solid hours, each journey — from Longueval to Bernafay Wood — being a distance of about 1 ½ miles. What food we had consisted of bits of biscuit which we found lying alongside dead bodies, and we never had a single rest during that time.*'

This man was himself shortly afterwards evacuated as a casualty. In the end indeed, there were no bearers left, and the wounded had simply to remain where they fell, or make their own way, if they could, to the dressing stations.

Meanwhile, nine crack German battalions were being massed on the perimeter for a determined thrust the moment the bom-

Left: Shell-shattered Delville Wood as it was in September 1916.

Below left: Delville Wood 1971, at the junction of two rides, Princes Street and Regent Street. At the time the undergrowth was being cleared, revealing large numbers of shell-holes.

Below right: A couple of newly-weds stroll in front of the South African memorial in Delville Wood. Their happiness makes a bitter contrast to earlier events in the same place.

bardment ended. These troops marvelled at the Verwüstunsfeuer before them, and doubted whether anyone could have survived such a storm.

At 3.30 p.m. the bombardment suddenly stopped, and the great attack began. To the astonishment of the oncoming German infantry, a handful of South Africans had not only survived, but, fatigued and shaken though they were, were clearly determined to let no one pass. The official German history describes the fight that followed as 'extremely terrible.' With rifle fire alone the South Africans repulsed attack after attack, and, when their ammunition gave out, they charged to their deaths with bayonets fixed. A German officer, describing the scene after the perimeter had been taken, noted sombrely in his diary:

'The wood was a wasteland of shattered trees, charred and burning stumps, craters thick with mud and blood, and corpses, corpses, everywhere. In places they were piled four deep. Worst of all was the lowing of the wounded. It sounded like a cattle ring at the spring fair.'

As dusk gathered, the chaos in the wood increased. Isolated individuals and small parties of Germans and South Africans found themselves hoplessly lost amid the tangle of wreckage and smoke. The historian of the German 52nd Infantry Regiment depicted the scene as one of 'indescribable confusion.'

As many South Africans as could filtered back to the centre of the wood where Col. Thackeray had established a strong-point at the intersection of two rides, nicknamed by the soldiers Rotten Row and Buchanan Street. Here they combined to make a stand, and shoulder to shoulder fought throughout the long hours of the 19th and 20th to prevent the German infantry from consolidating their hold on the wood.

And in this they succeeded.

The measure of their achievement can perhaps best be gauged by the fact that 'Devil's Wood', as it came to be known to friend and foe alike, was not eventually recaptured in its entirety by the British until some six weeks later. When the dead came to be buried, the bodies of only 142 out of the many South Africans who had fallen were recovered, and of these only 77 could be identified.

The significance of their stand was fully appreciated by the commanders on both sides. Had they given way, there is little doubt that the second phase of the Somme offensive — of which the battle for Delville Wood formed a part — would have ended in disaster. The operations then beginning against Ginchy on the one side and High Wood on the other would have been hopelessly outflanked. The British supply lines, at that stage unprotected by any substantial force, would have lain wide open to a crippling thrust. The whole Somme offensive, indeed, might have been thrown off balance, necessitating a retreat from the ground so expensively gained. It would not be an exaggeration to say that for three days the South African infantry brigade held the fortune of Haig's "Big Push" in its hands.

It was not found wanting.

British Army boot fragment discovered in High Wood by John Giles.

HIGH WOOD

High Wood, like its nearby counterpart Delville Wood, was to become one of the most ghastly areas of the whole Somme offensive. Before the attack of 14th July it was just a wood; by the time it was captured, two months later, it was unrecognisable. Strategically situated on the brow of a hill, the Germans fought ferociously to retain it within their defensive network. In fact the bloodshed need not have happened, for immediately after the early success of the dawn attack of 14th July, this front appeared to be wide open. Several senior officers walked up the slope seen in the photograph facing and were not shot at; they saw no enemy troops or defensive works. In consequence the commanders of 7th and 3rd Divisions wanted to seize the opportunity and advance, but they were prevented by higher authority. The reason was that cavalry had been allotted the task. But the cavalry did not arrive on the scene until very late and the chance was lost. Moreover, an attempt by the cavalry to obtain a breakthrough later in the day was beaten back by machine-gun fire.

Desperate fighting subsequently went on almost continuously for two months, until the Battle of Flers-Courcelette on 15th September 1916, when the shattered wood fell to troops of the 47th (London) Division, but even then not without bloody and close fighting. Before that four other divisions had all suffered heavy losses there.

The extract on the right, taken from a story told by one who was there, portrays the horror of the fierce fighting for the wood.

Above right: High Wood after its capture by the 47th Division on 15th September 1916. On the right a gun team of the 2nd Battery, New Zealand Field Artillery is going forward. The photograph appears to have been taken on the open ground at the right of the wood.

Imperial War Museum

"Tighten up your belts, lads," I ordered. "We're going to advance." Then I rose. With a swift rush we swept forward, the softness of bodies yielding in our step. A wounded man called to me, his plaintiff wail tearing the heart. I dammed the source of my compassion, and set myself to the purpose of the moment, then again dropped for cover and rest. No shot was fired. A third rush. The party on its narrow front in a thin irregular line was within forty yards of the wood's edge. I whispered the words to left and to right, "Fix bayonets." Once more my lads rose from the blood-soaked fields in a mad rush.

If there had been any martyr in my soul it had turned beast. I was murderer, breath coming in short gasps, teeth set, hands clenched round my rifle, nerves and sinews tense with life. "An eye for an eye, a tooth for a tooth." Four German soldiers raised their arms in surrender. I could hear the breath of the sergeant coming in deep snarles beside me. I crashed through the undergrowth, rifle and bayonet levelled to the charge, my great strength and weight gathered behind the thrust. A man, bearded and begrimed with battle, crumpled before my bayonet. The sergeant pierced another as a knife goes through butter. A soldier, his arm broken, cowered back against a machine-gun, hands raised, face blanched with terror. With a cry he turned to run. I thrust with my bayonet at the full extent of a strong arm. The man stumbled and fell back. his weight dragging the rifle from the hand of his slayer.
Graham Seton Hutchison

76

Above: This photograph, taken in 1974, gives a good idea of the magnitude of the task confronting our troops at High Wood. In the centre foreground is Thistle Dump Military Cemetery.

Left: The Somme with High Wood in the background. L-R: The author; ex-Captain 'GB' Jameson, R.F.A., M.C., aged 93; The Countess Haig; The Earl Haig, O.B.E., K.St.J., D.L.; former Private W. E. 'Josh' Grover, M.M., 2nd Battalion, Royal Sussex, aged 89; and former Private Harry Goodby, London Scottish, aged 88. 'Josh' Grover was in action on the right of High Wood (in the capture of Wood Trench) in September 1916. This picture was taken at Easter 1984.

The sergeant ordered me to search the dug-outs for prisoners and the very first one contained two officers, one NCO and one signaller. Each one had a loaded revolver and they could have shot me had they wanted to. I disarmed them and they seemed to be pleased at being made prisoner. When I got them into open ground a young lad, who had joined us while being under age, came along and went berserk. He shot one of the officers and when I called on him to stop he ran on towards the German lines. He was later reported as being missing. I took the prisoners to the rear and before they left me the other officer gave me his Iron Cross.

H. A. Boyce

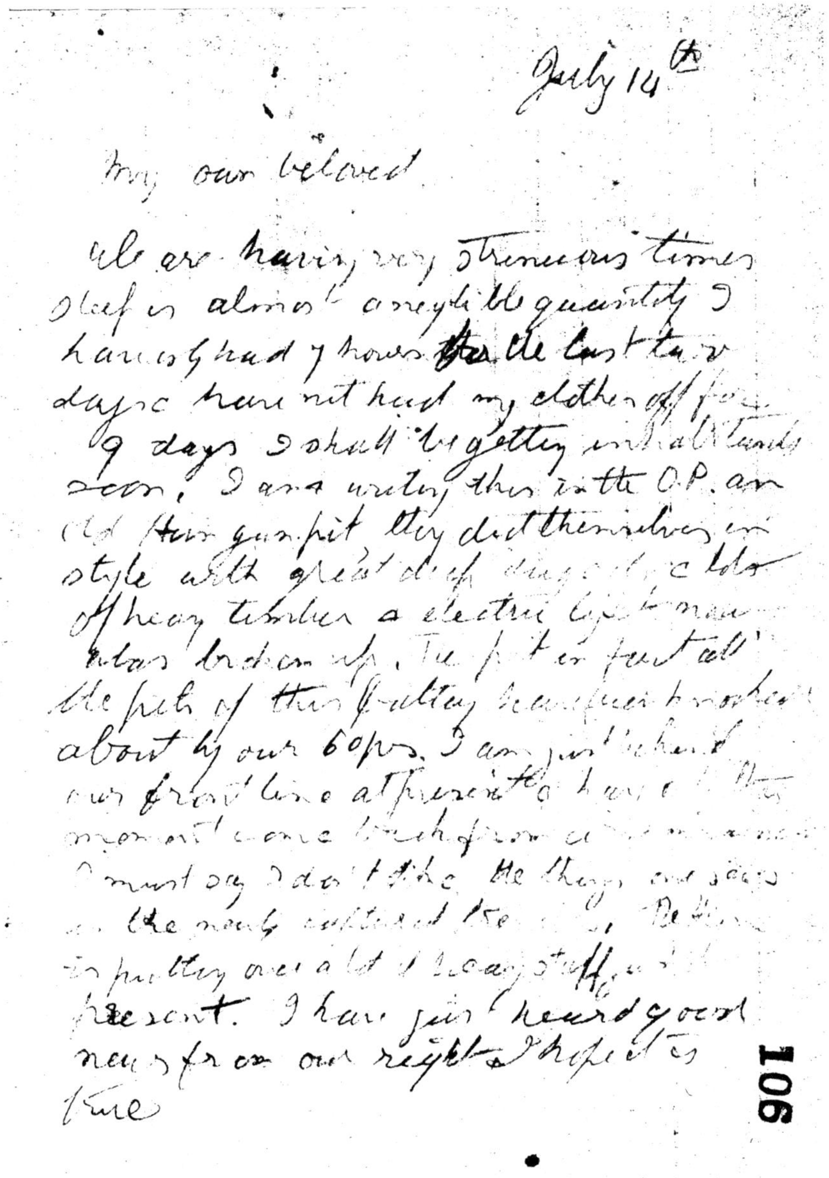

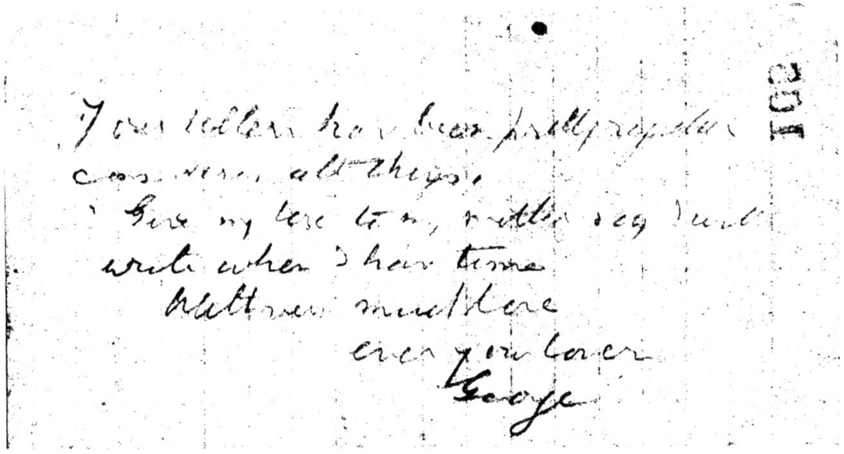

July 14th

My own beloved,

We are having very strenuous times, sleep is almost a negligible quantity. I have only had 7 hours for the last two days and have not had my clothes off for 9 days. I shall be getting inhabitants soon. I am writing this in the O.P., an old Hun gunpit; they did themselves in style with great deep dugouts and lots of heavy timber and electric light, now alas broken up. The pit, in fact all the pits of this battery, have been knocked about by our 60pdrs. I am just behind our front line at present and have only this moment come back from a reconnaisance. I must say I don't like the things one sees in the newly captured trenches. The Hun is putting over a lot of heavy stuff just at present. I have just heard good news from our right. I hope it is true. Your letters have been pretty regular considering all things. Give my love to my mother. I will write when I have time.

With very much love,
Ever your lover,
George.

The last letter, written in pencil on the page of an army notebook by Major G. F. Farran, Royal Artillery, to his wife, a few days before he was killed in Bailiff Wood, near Contalmaison (18th July 1916).

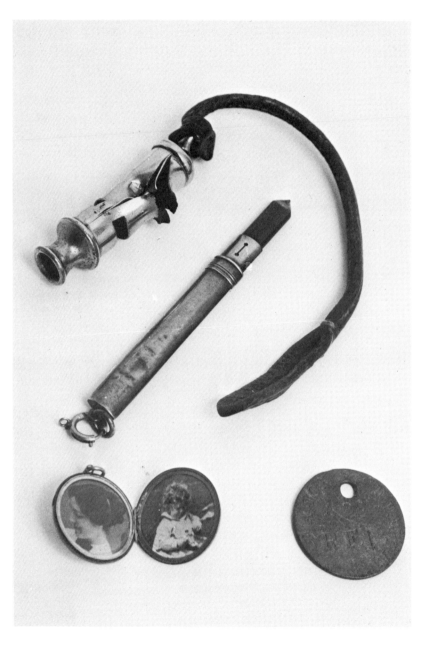

Above: A pre-war photograph of Major Farran, taken when he held the rank of captain.

Right: Major Farran's effects: his identity disc, a silver pencil, a gold locket containing pictures of his wife and small daughter, and his whistle, damaged by the shrapnel ball which is believed to have killed him.

WATERLOT FARM

This powerful enemy strongpoint — a former sugar refinery — was located on the German second line between Longueval and Guillemont. From there it commanded the southern approaches to Delville Wood and also the village of Longueval itself.

Fierce fighting took place around the position and repeated attempts had to be made before the defenders were finally driven out.

The main task of capturing this stronghold fell to the 26th Brigade of the 9th Division from which a company of the 5th Cameron Highlanders advanced at dawn on the 15th July. These men, who were later supported by units of the 4th South African Regiment, attacked the farm time and time again and eventually succeeded in ejecting the Germans.

But owing to a heavy enemy bombardment, it was not until the morning of 17th July that our troops completed its capture.

Above left: Site of Waterlot Farm, near Ginchy on the Guillemont road, July 1916.

Below left: Waterlot Farm, July 1971.

POZIÈRES

This village, astride the main Albert—Bapaume road and less than four miles from the former, was situated on a ridge that commanded a very wide area of the main battleground. It was a short distance in front of the German second line defences and was itself protected by deep trenches, masses of barbed wire and numerous machine-gun posts located in cellars of houses and other vantage points. Just beyond the eastern end of the village, on a knoll, was situated what had once been a windmill. The upper part had been destroyed by shell fire; the base had been converted by the enemy into a veritable fortress of concrete packed with machine-guns. This was the highest point on the Pozières Ridge and was of immense strategical value for, apart from the superb observation over miles of open country, it controlled the main road to Bapaume and covered the rear approaches to the Thiepval Plateau. Thiepval had proved too hard a nut to crack by a frontal assault, and after the failure of 1st July, it became Haig's intention to drive on it from the rear, thus causing the enemy to abandon one of the strongest portions of his original line.

In the early optimistic days preceeding the opening of the Somme offensive, it had been hoped — even expected — that Pozières would fall on the first day of the battle. Indeed, men of the 8th Division were led to believe that they would reach the village without undue difficulty by the afternoon of that same day. Events, however, proved otherwise, and it was over three weeks later before most of Pozières fell to troops of the 1st Anzac Corps after extremely fierce fighting.

Below: The badly shelled road to Bapaume, through Pozières, 20th September 1916, showing a communication trench in the foreground.

Below left: The same main road in July 1971. The road from Thiepval enters the village about half way through on the left and on the right is a road to Bazentin le Petit. Beyond the end of the village is the former site of the windmill. Close to where this picture was taken was a German strongpoint known as Gibralter.

Imperial War Museum

. . . We had now reached the outskirts of the village . . . This was it. Everything seemed to be going up around us. We passed the first crumbled walls of houses, against which bullets were spattering like hailstones. Men were hardly discernable in the darkness. Lashed by sprays of dust and broken brick, we stumbled over stones and plunged into shell-holes. I hopped from place to place, zigzagging with the shelling, following first one man and then another. Everything was blurred. My throat was parched, my eyes full of water. We ran into a hail of bullets as we struck some cobble-stones which must have been the main road. The men staggered across it, all lit up by the glare from Verey lights. I managed to scrape under the lee of an old capsized ambulance-cart, though bullets were ripping through it as though it had been brown paper. Then our progress slowed down.

Paul Maze

These veterans of Gallipoli had recently come down from Flanders and had then been placed under the direction of General Gough's Reserve (Fifth) Army which had the task of capturing Pozières and the ridge. The 48th Division of X Corps was to co-operate on the left of the Australians, with the date of the overall attack being fixed for 23rd July. Zero hour was 12.30 a.m.

With great dash and courage the 1st Australian Division assaulted in the blackness of a night lit up by shell-bursts and enemy flares. Vicious fighting took place amongst the ruins of houses and in cellars but within a short time the axis of the main road was reached and the men dug in under a furious enemy bombardment. During daylight on the 23rd the line was pushed forward, although on the left the 48th Division had met with a rebuff.

Further bitter fighting took place around Pozières on the 25th with a terrible concentration of artillery fire being directed on the attackers. Casualties mounted alarmingly, and the 1st Australian Division was withdrawn, having suffered over 5,000 losses. Its place was taken by the 2nd Australian Divison which in turn was drawn into the maelstrom as further attempts were made to push forward in the direction of Mouquet Farm. By the 29th July this division had incurred nearly 3,500 casualties.

Another major attack was mounted at 9.15 p.m. on the 4th August with fierce hand-to-hand fighting taking place. British units of 12th Division successfully co-operated on the left flank,

Above right: Remains of the windmill and general view of the devastated condition of the area, October 1916.

Below right: The grassy site of the windmill, July 1973. The low, concrete tablet at the end of the path is inscribed with the following words:

> 'THE RUIN OF POZIERES WINDMILL WHICH LIES HERE WAS THE CENTRE OF THE STRUGGLE IN THIS PART OF THE SOMME BATTLEFIELD IN JULY AND AUGUST 1916. IT WAS CAPTURED ON AUGUST 4th BY AUSTRALIAN TROOPS WHO FELL MORE THICKLY ON THIS RIDGE THAN ON ANY OTHER BATTLEFIELD OF THE WAR.'

Traces of the concrete machine-gun fortifications beneath the windmill can still be seen.

With the same untiring regularity explosion after explosion shook the ridge. I looked over the rim of our shelter as shells turned the earth like rough seas, and saw bodies lying about as though drifting after a wreck. Here and there only hands could be seen, flung up with the final gesture of drowning men . . . The ground was so thickly littered with broken bricks that the battle might have been fought with them. Field-dressings were strewn all over the place. Some German dead were still clasping their hand-grenades. Near us an Australian and a German, killed at the moment they had come to grips, hung together on the parapet like marionettes embracing each other . . . The smell of decomposition everywhere was very trying. In places human remains appeared, gruesomely forming part of the parapets . . . It suddenly dawned on me that this was the remains of the windmill, which had cost us countless lives . . .

Paul Maze

and our artillery pounded the German defences with a heavy bombardment. Enemy counter-attacks developed but were smashed by machine-gun and artillery fire. Early on the 5th August Australian troops were dug in round the site of the windmill with observation towards Courcelette, Mouquet Farm and Thiepval Ridge. A major part of the German second line trenches had fallen, but the cost had been very heavy. Even then there was no respite for the men, for there followed a period of most terrible fighting together with devastating enemy artillery fire as the line was consolidated and then painfully pushed forward.

Pozières is a name that will live in Australian history as a place of carnage where bravery and tenacity were bywords. This was principally an Australian 'show' where men from the old Commonwealth demonstrated their capacity to take it and give it in no uncertain fashion.

Imperial War Museum

Above left: The civilian cemetery, on the outskirts of Pozières and along the Thiepval road, was the scene of bitter fighting in July 1916. Both front lines were at one time located there, very close to each other. The area was captured on 29th July by troops of the Australian Brigade. Unfortunately they suffered heavy casualties through being hit by their own barrage after having advanced beyond their original objective which had been obliterated by shell fire.

Below left: The cemetery as it is today.

Above: Two skulls, one in British steel helmet, discovered on the former battlefield of Pozières after the First World War. The picture was supplied by Madame Rabatel-Goullieux Dargis, a former Paris Opera singer who lived in Pozières as a child. She recollects returning to the village when the war ended and finding it razed to the ground.

To be able to walk through Pozières and not to be shelled was an odd sensation. Nothing remained of the village; it had been pulverised. Somehow, something attached me to the place. Crosses were sticking out of the churned-up ground like daffodils in a wood in spring . . . As a consolation I could read as many German names as ours on the crosses . . .

Paul Maze

Imperial War Museum

Left: This view of the Pozières battlefield, as it was on 20th April 1917, and showing thousands upon thousands of overlapping shell-holes, is reminiscent of the dreadful quagmires of Passchendaele, in the following November.

Below: The immense open aspect of the old Pozières battlefield, July 1974, looking towards the Thiepval Ridge and with the memorial left of centre. Its capture claimed the lives of very many soldiers, numbers of whom now rest in Pozières Military Cemetery, close to which this photograph was taken.

We came to a thinly-held trench, which surprisingly escaped being bombarded, and followed it up to where it jutted out into the cemetery, most of which was still held by the enemy; as I looked up, the tops of shattered marble pillars and bead wreaths appeared all round. The very front post, unshelled in the midst of this wild bombardment, felt like a calm backwater of a whirling pool. Men talked in hushed voices, as though they wanted to keep the secret of their sanctuary. One of them whispered: "Fritz is there in the old bone-yard, about ten yards away; if you look up you'll see some of them moving about the communication trench . . . The doubts entertained by the artillery of both sides as to who was actually in the cemetery accounted for this peaceful gap only a yard or two from the enemy.

Paul Maze

84

GUILLEMONT

As July came to an end and the great offensive moved into its second month, it became obvious to the British military leaders that the hoped-for breakthrough was not likely to occur in the immediate future. Sir Douglas Haig therefore changed his tactics with a view to wearing down the enemy while at the same time husbanding his own strength in men and materials preparatory to a possible further major effort in September. He also planned to give support to the French on the right flank and this entailed the capture of Guillemont and Ginchy by the Fourth Army. On its left the Reserve Army was to undertake limited actions, in the area of Mouquet Farm.

General Rawlinson and General Fayolle, commander of the French Sixth Army, finally agreed upon a combined attack for the 8th August. In the British sector, the 55th Division and 2nd Division, both of XIII Corps, were to be involved, with the village and the open ground up to Waterlot Farm being the objectives.

At 4.20 a.m. on the appointed day the infantry jumped off under heavy bombardment from German guns. Desperate fighting occurred, and at one point the ruins of Guillemont were entered by the Liverpool Irish of 164th Brigade. Elsewhere on the front of the 55th Division the attack was checked by fierce enemy resistance. To the north a temporary success was gained by the 2nd Division, but there also the attack fizzled out with heavy losses.

Next morning the attack was renewed but once again no real headway was made. Terrible hand-to-hand struggles took place in Guillemont, the station and a nearby quarry; but gradually the situation worsened, and by late evening our forward troops had been overwhelmed. That same night the 2nd Division was relieved by the 24th Division, having suffered nearly 5,000 casualties.

In spite of these set-backs General Haig insisted on pressure being maintained in order, he intimated, to assist our Russian Allies (who were meeting with considerable success at that time on the Eastern front) and, of course, the French on our right. What he appeared to overlook was the dreadful problem of overcoming the numerous German machine-guns dotted about in shell-holes

and the rubble of Guillemont. He also suggested that the commander and other senior officers of XIII Corps 'needed a rest' and in fact, on the 10th August, Lieut.-Gen. W. N. Congreve was relieved of his corps command, to be replaced by Lieut.-Gen. the Earl of Cavan, former commander of XIV Corps. Other officers from the latter corps also began to take over the posts of Congreve's staff and, a few days later, this right hand corps of Fourth Army was styled XIV Corps.

Another combined British-French attack was planned for 11th August but was postponed for twenty-four hours. Once again too this attempt met with failure in the British sector and only partial success on the French right flank (their left also being held up).

Above: German dead behind a smashed-up machine-gun post, near Guillemont, September 1916.

The horrible aspect of the Sunken Road — a series of huge shell-holes, filled with uniforms, equipment, arms and dead bodies. A dreadful place — the dead defenders lay amongst the living. Whilst digging funk-holes we discovered that they had been buried in strata. One company after another had crowded in and been destroyed by drum fire. The Sunken Road and the ground in rear of it were full of Germans; the ground in front was strewn with British dead.

F. C. Hitchcock.

Imperial War Museum

Above right: General view of the battlefield at Guillemont, September 1916. Bodies, and bits of bodies, lie in profusion across the desolate ground with, near the centre, what appears to be a pair of booted legs protruding upside down from a shell-hole or what was once a trench.

Below right: Part of the old Guillemont battlefield, July 1973. The spire of Longeuval church is on the extreme left, Guillemont Station (light railway) would have been in the centre distance and Guillemont church is on the right. This picture was taken from near Trones Wood, and the countours of the ground suggest that the war-time photograph above was also taken from the same position.

On this side of the church can be seen the Cross of Sacrifice of Guillemont Military Cemetery, in which is buried a son of Mr. Asquith, British Prime Minister at the time of the Somme offensive.

Pressure then came from General Joffre to widen the sphere of action and a meeting took place between the Commanders-in-Chief on the 12th August at Beauquesne. From this it was agreed that the whole line between the Somme and High Wood — including Guillemont — would be attacked on the 18th August.

Meanwhile the 55th Division was relieved by the 3rd Division after having incurred over 4,000 casualties.

On the 18th the main assault continued and everywhere it became the same story of carnage. New attacks were mounted in the Guillemont area on the 21st August and on the 24th the French completed the capture of Maurepass. Bitter engagements continued as August drew to a close and fresh plans were made for September.

On the 3rd September began the final assault on what was left of Guillemont. The task was given to the 20th (Light) Division which had already been severely mauled in previous operations. Indeed for that reason it was necessary to relieve the 60th Brigade, and its place was taken by the 47th Brigade from the 16th (Irish) Division.

By 12.30 p.m. the first objectives were taken with the Irish in particular attacking with great vigour. As the afternoon drew on the site of Guillemont was firmly in our possession in spite of considerable enemy machine-gun and artillery fire. The overall cost in lives for the capture of this destroyed village had, however, been frightening.

Imperial War Museum

Above right: The road to Guillemont, September 1916. The village itself was obliterated.

Below right: Entrance to Guillemont village fifty-five years later.

Just above us on the parapet a group of German dead were lying heaped up, swollen and festering with clouds of fat, blowsy flies buzzing all over them. Big, hefty looking fellows: all youngsters, hardly a bearded face amongst them. More bodies in odd corners of the trench itself, in between the sandbags, trampled in the muck and mud of the floor, on the parados. There had been heavy scrapping here. This shallow ditch had changed hands two or three times during the last four days, and there had been no time to remove the fallen.

Giles Eyre.

Imperial War Museum

Above and left: Two pictures which portray some of the horrors of the battlefield as the offensive ground on.

Imperial War Museum

88

GUILLEMONT

By Lieut. Ernst Junger, 73rd
Hanoverian Fusilier Regiment.

Hundreds of heavy batteries were concentrated on and round Combles. Innumerable shells came howling and hurtling over us. Thick smoke, ominously lit up by Verey lights, veiled everything. Head and ears ached violently, and we could only make ourselves understood by shouting a word at a time. The power of logical thought and the force of gravity seemed alike to be suspended. One had the sense of something as unescapable and as unconditionally fated as a catastrophe of nature. A N.C.O. of No.3 platoon went mad.

At 10 this carnival of hell gradually calmed down and passed into a steady drum-fire. It was still certainly impossible to distinguish one shell from another.

At 11 orders came to parade in the square. There we joined the other two platoons preparatory to marching into the line. There was a fourth platoon under Lieutenant Sievers detailed to carry rations forward. They surrounded us while we were hastily got together on this risky spot, and loaded us with things to eat, of which in those days there were still plentiful supplies. Sievers pressed a pan full of butter on me, and shaking my hand at parting wished me luck.

Then we moved off in single file. Every man had the strictest orders to follow closely on the man in front. We had scarcely got out of the place before the guide found he had missed the way. We were compelled to turn back under heavy shrapnel fire. Next we were following, mostly at the double, a white band laid down over the open ground to give the direction. It was shot into small bits. Often we had to come to a halt at the worst moment, when our guide lost his way. To lie down was forbidden, in case we lost touch.

In spite of this, Nos. 1 and 3 platoons suddenly vanished. On again! We got to a sunken road, much shelled, where the sections stowed themselves. 'Lie down' was the order. A nauseous and oppressive scent warned us that this road had claimed many a victim. After a run that threatened death at every step we reached a second sunken road in which battle headquarters were concealed. Then we went the wrong way and had to turn back, nerve-racked and crowding on each other. Five metres, at the utmost, from Vogel and myself a medium-heavy shell struck the rear bank of the road will a dull crash and shot a volley of great clods on us, while its deadly fragments flew in a shower over our backs. At last the guide found the way again. He had come upon a surprising landmark — a group of dead bodies.

On and on! Some of the men collapsed as they ran, for we were compelled to force the last ounce from their exhausted bodies. Wounded men called to us on left and right from the shell-holes and were disregarded. On and on, with our eyes fixed on the man in front, along a knee-deep trench formed of linked-up shell-holes of enormous size, where the dead were almost touching. Our feet found little purchase against their soft and yielding bodies. Even the wounded who fell by the way shared the same fate and were trodden beneath the boots of those who still hurried on.

And always this sickly smell. Even my orderly, little Schmidt, my companion in many a dangerous patrol, began to reel. I snatched the rifle from his hand, though even at such a moment his politeness made him resist me.

At last we reached the front line. It was held by men cowering close in the shell-holes, and their dead voices trembled with joy when they heard that we were the relief. A Bavarian sergeant-major briefly handed over the sector and the Verey-light pistol.

My platoon front formed the right wing of the position held by the regiment. It consisted of a shallow sunken road which had been pounded by shells. It was a few hundred metres left of Guillemont and a rather shorter distance right of Bois-de-Trones. We were parted from the troops on our right, the 76th Regiment of Infantry, by a space about 500 metres wide. This space was shelled so violently that no troops could maintain themselves there.

The Bavarian sergeant-major had vanished of a sudden and I stood alone, the Verey-light pistol in my hand, in the midst of an uncanny sea of shell-holes over which lay a white mist whose swathes gave it an even more oppressive and mysterious appearance. A persistent, unpleasant smell came from behind. I was left in no doubt that it came from a gigantic corpse far gone in decay.

As I had no idea how far off the enemy were, I warned my men to be ready for the worst. We all remained on guard. I spent the night with my batman and two orderlies in a hole perhaps one yard square and one yard deep.

When day dawned we were astonished to see, by degrees, what a sight surrounded us.

The sunken road now appeared as nothing but a series of enormous shell-holes filled with pieces of uniform, weapons, and dead bodies. The ground all round, as far as the eye could see, was ploughed by shells. You could search in vain for one wretched blade of grass. This churned-up battlefield was ghastly. Among the living lay the dead. As we dug ourselves in we found them in layers stacked one upon the top of another. One company after another had been shoved into the drum-fire and steadily annihilated. The corpses were covered with the masses of soil turned up by the shells, and the next company advanced in the place of the fallen.

The sunken road and the ground behind was full of German dead; the ground in front of English. Arms, legs, and head stuck out stark above the lips of the craters. In front of our miserable defences there were torn-off limbs and corpses over many of which cloaks and ground-sheets had been thrown to hide the fixed stare of their distorted features. In spite of the heat no one thought for a moment of covering them with soil.

The village of Guillemont was distinguished from the landscape around it only because the shell-holes there were of a whiter colour by reason of the houses which had been ground to powder. Guillemont railway station lay in front of us. It was smashed to bits like a child's plaything. Delville wood, reduced to matchwood, was further behind.

Day had scarcely dawned when an English flying-man descended on us in a steep spin and circled round incessantly like a bird of prey. while we made for our holes and cowered there. Nevertheless, the observer's sharp eyes must have spied us out, for a siren sounded its deep long-drawn notes above us at short intervals. After a little while it appeared that a battery had received the signal. One heavy shell after another came at us on a flat trajectory with incredible fury. We crouched in our refuges and could do nothing. Now and then we lit a cigar and threw it away again. Every moment we expected a rush of earth to bury us. The sleeve of Schmidt's coat was torn by a big splinter.

At the third shot the occupant of the next hole to mine was buried by a terrific explosion. We dug him out instantly, but the weight of earth had killed him. His face had fallen in and looked like a death's head. It was the volunteer Simon. Tribulation had made him wise. Whenever in the course of the day, when airmen were about, any one stirred from his cover, Simon was heard scolding and his warning fist appeared from behind the ground-sheet that curtained his earth.

At three in the afternoon the men came in from the left flank and said they could stick it no longer as their shelters were shot to bits. It cost me all my callousness to get them back to their posts.

Just before ten at night the left flank of the regimental front was heavily shelled, and after twenty minutes we came in for it too. In a brief space we were completely covered in dust and smoke, and yet most of the hits were just in front or just behind. While this hurricane was raging I went along my platoon front. The men were standing, rifle in hand, as though carved in stone, their eyes fixed on the ground in front of them. Now and then by the light of a rocket I saw the gleam of helmet after helmet, bayonet after bayonet, and I was filled with pride at commanding this handful of men that might very likely be pounded into the earth but could not be conquered. It is in such moments that the human spirit triumphs over the mightiest demonstrations of material force. The fragile body, steeled by the will, stands up to the most terrific punishment.Sergeant-major H., the unfortunate rat-catcher of Monchy, who was with the platoon on our left, intended to fire a white Very light. By mistake he fired a red one, and this signal was taken up on all sides. At once our barrage came down to a tune which delighted us. One shell after another went howling over our heads and crashed in sparks and splinters over the ground in front of us. A mixture of dust, suffocating gases, and vaporous exhalations of corpses flung high in the air was blown back on us from the shell-holes. After this orgy of destruction, the fire returned to its customary level and stayed there all the night and the next day. One man in a moment of agitation had released the whole mighty machinery of war.

H. remained what he was, an unlucky fellow. That same night he shot a Verey light into the leg of his boot while loading the pistol, and had to be carried back severely burnt. Next day it rained hard, and we were not sorry. With the laying of the dust the parched feeling was relieved and the great clusters of blue-bottles which the sun had brought out were driven away. I sat nearly all day in front of my earth on the ground, smoking, and eating, too, with appetite, in spite of my surroundings.

The next morning, Fusilier Knicke of my platoon got a bullet from somewhere through the chest. It hit the spine too and paralysed his legs. When I went to see him he was lying in one of the shelter-holes quite resigned. In the evening when he was being carried back he had a leg broken on one of the many occasions when his bearers had to take cover from the shell-fire. He died at the dressing-station.

At mid-day a man of my platoon got me to have a shot at a single Englishman in Guillemont railway station. When I looked I saw hundreds of English hurrying forward along a shallow communication trench. They were not particularly upset by the rifle-fire we could bring to bear on them. This sight showed the unequal terms on which we fought, for if we had ventured on anything like it our men would have been shot to pieces in a few minutes. While on our side not a captive balloon was to be seen, on the English side there were thirty at once over one spot, observing every movement with argus eyes and at once directing a hail of iron upon it.

In the evening a big shell-splinter came hurtling for my stomach, but fortunately it was pretty well spent and fell to the ground after striking the buckle of my belt.

Two members of an English ration-party who had lost their way appeared at dusk on No. 1 platoon front. Both were shot down at point-blank range. One of them fell half into the sunken road, while his legs remained on the top of the ditch. None of the men would take prisoners, for how could we get them through the barrage? It was bad enough on our own without prisoners to see to.

Towards one in the morning I was roused from a confused sleep by Schmidt. I jumped up nervously and seized my rifle. It was our relief. We handed over what there was to hand over, and departed with all speed from this corner of hell.

We had scarcely reached the shallow communication trench when the first group of shrapnel burst among us. The man in front of me reeled from a wound in the wrist from which the blood spurted. He wanted to fall out and lie down. I caught him by the arm and got him to his feet in spite of his dazed condition, and did not let him go till I handed him over in the dressing-station near battle headquarters.

It was hot work in both of the sunken roads, and we got quite out of breath. The tightest corner of all was when we found ourselves in a hollow where shrapnel and light shells were coming over all the time . . . Brruch! Brruch! the rain of iron crashed round us, scattering a shower of sparks in the darkness. Whoee! Another volley! . . . the soft earth was flung high. This one of all others was a dud. A better opportunity could not be wished for making the influence of an officer tell. Everywhere relieved and reliefs were hurrying through the shells and the darkness, some of them utterly lost and dazed with excitement and exhaustion. Everywhere voices rang out, in command, or in monotonous supplication from the shell-holes where the wounded were left to their fate. As we rushed by, I gave information to those who had lost their way, pulled men out of shell-holes, threatened to shoot any who wanted to fall out, kept shouting my name to keep my men together, and at last, as though by a miracle, I got my platoon back to Combles.

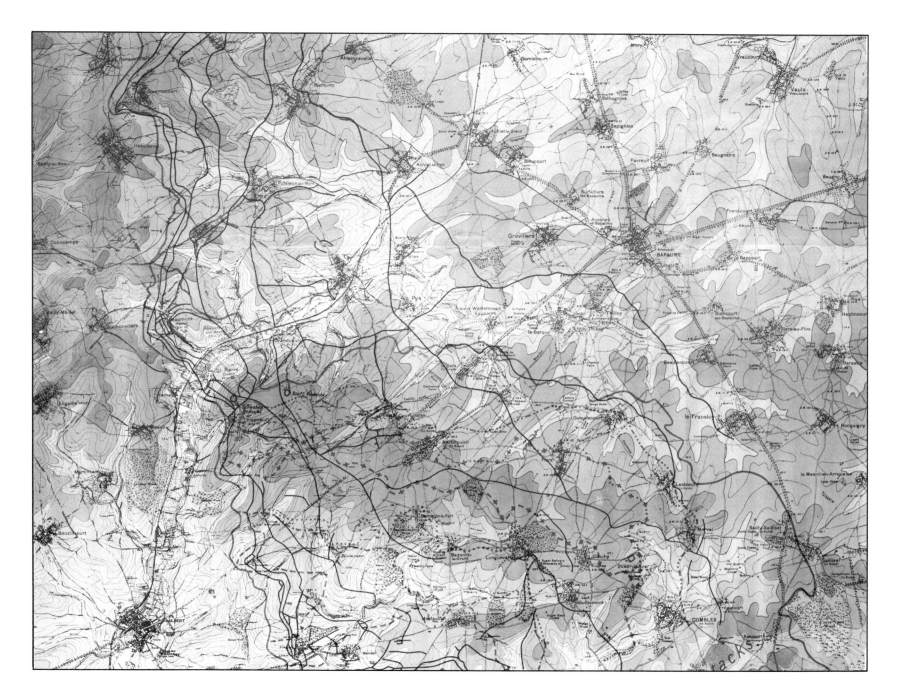

GINCHY

Ginchy lay just a short distance to the north-east of Guillemont and close to the south-eastern corner of Delville Wood. Its capture was included in the planned assault of 3rd September and the task was to be undertaken by the 7th Divison of XV Corps.

At noon on that day units of 22nd Brigade dashed forward and swept into the southern portion of the village. On the left flank, however, the advance was held up by machine-gun fire, with heavy losses. Some men nevertheless got into the northern part of the village but then disappeared. A German flank counter-attack developed which caused a necessary retirement although some parties of troops still held out. Attempts by the Royal Irish to press forward were disorganised by enemy shelling.

At 8 a.m. on the 4th September the 9th Devons of 20th Brigade went over the top and got into Ginchy, where the battalion ran into a storm of machine-gun fire which forced them to withdraw after having received considerable losses. Due to further set-backs it was decided that a night-time assault would achieve better results. Consequently in the early morning of 6th September, and under cover of darkness, the 2nd Gordon Highlanders went forward towards their objective. The darkness caused some confusion so the Gordons, in company with the 9th Devons, tried again at 5.30 a.m. with little better result. At 2 p.m. they tried yet again and although initially successful they and the Devons had to withdraw after having got into the village because of an enemy barrage and counter-attack. By then Ginchy, like Guillemont, had practically ceased to exist due to the repeated bombardments of both British and German guns.

The next major attack on Ginchy was fixed for the 9th September and by then the capture of the village had become the responsibility of XIV Corps, with the 16th Division to deliver the main blow.

Imperial War Museum

Above: Ginchy in September 1916; the mound of bricks and rubble on the right was probably the church.

Below: Ginchy in July 1973.

Opposite: The front lines — 31st August.

At 4.45 p.m. troops of the 48th Brigade advanced and in spite of some checks they and other Irish soldiers who were attached from two battalions of 49th Brigade streamed through the ruined village and beyond, causing many of the enemy to fly towards Flers whilst others were captured.

The 16th Division suffered a total of over 4,300 casualties between 1st-10th September.

Above: The legend on the board reads 'RIP Corporal 6th Connaught Rangers. Name unknown. Killed 15th September 1916'. It was a common practice to mark graves with rifles embedded in the ground by the bayonet, to help burial parties later. However, shell fire often obliterated them so that the body became lost, in many cases for ever.

Right: A wrecked German trench at Ginchy, September 1916, with new occupants. The weight of the British bombardment is illustrated by the state of the trees.

Imperial War Museum

I was borne to a Casualty Clearing Station but I had to wait my turn for a vacant bed. Wounded were being cleared as fast as surgeons in their shirt-sleeves could accomplish their work. But speedy as were the butchers, death was faster still and left ample space for incomers.

British and Germans were treated alike; and beside me lay a young Bavarian, his chin still hairless, one of the Alpine Corps, from mountains I knew and loved, with a shattered thigh and other grievous injuries. His face was pale, and the eyes very bright. Orderlies and nurses looked at him every now and again to see how he fared. And while others groaned, and some shrieked with agony, he never uttered a sound. Only when night fell and the lamps were lighted did he begin to whimper quietly. His hand lay stretched out over the coverlet. I sometimes glanced at the lad. He was crying like a child, so I touched his hand, and he held on. I think that made his passage easier, for he sighed and smiled at me, and a little later he slept. Then they took the body away.

Graham Seton Hutchison

Above: A badly wounded German waiting to be moved from the battleground.

Above right: A wounded British soldier being taken from the battlefield after the capture of Ginchy, September 1916. Note the horse smothered in bluebottles, and the tape marking the route.

Imperial War Museum

95

THE DEBUT OF THE TANKS

The evolution of the 'Tank' (so named for security reasons) stemmed mainly from Winston Churchill when he was First Lord of the Admiralty. In spite of a lack of enthusiasm in high Army circles, he allotted, on his own responsibility, Admiralty funds for research into 'land battleships'. In January 1915 he sanctioned the formation of a 'Landship Committee' to organise and control the development of a suitable machine, and in due course experiments were carried out, in strict secrecy, by the Armoured Car Division of the R.N.A.S.

Another enthusiast for the idea was Major (later to become Maj.-Gen. Sir) E. D. Swinton. As early as October 1914 he had submitted his plans, based on a cross-country tractor, to the Secretary of the War Council; but after minimum experiments the project was dropped. In June 1915, however, his detailed proposals were resuscitated, and the War Office approached the Admiralty with specific advice on what the Army requirements for such a machine would be.

Following the Gallipoli fiasco Churchill left the Admiralty, and Swinton — now a Colonel — became a prime mover of the project. Churchill, who was still a member of the War Committee, continued to do everything possible to help; and it was largely due to his driving force that the original idea became a reality.

At the beginning of February 1916 secret trials with an early 'tank' took place at Hatfield, witnessed by Lloyd George (then Minister of Munitions), Lord Kitchener and others of high rank. As a result, an order was placed for 100 of them, officially known as the Mark 1 Tank, and a new unit, the Heavy Branch, Machine-gun Corps, was formed to man them.

It was on these that Haig built his hopes for an autumn breakthrough. On 16th August he informed the Fourth and Reserve Armies of preliminary plans for a mid-September offensive in which, for the first time ever, tanks were to have a role. So sure was he that the Germans, through his wearing-down policy, would already be near breaking point, that he refused to wait for the new weapon to be ready in sufficient numbers.

At home it was considered that it would be better to delay. It was estimated that by January 1917 something like 500 machines with trained crews would be available. But Haig insisted on going ahead, and hoped for at least 50 tanks to be ready for the attack.

Meanwhile heavy fighting continued all along the main front during the remainder of August, including at High Wood and Delville Wood. Thousands of men perished in attack and counter-attack in storms of lead and steel for which flesh and blood were no match, but against which, it was fervently hoped by the few who knew about them, tanks might prove to be the answer.

Imperial War Museum

Above: The prototype of Marks 1, 2 and 3 series of tanks. The Mark 1 weighed 28 tons, was 26'5" in length, had a crew of eight, and a top speed of about 3½ m.p.h. on level ground. There were two types, known as the 'male' and the 'female'; the main armament of the former was two Hotchkiss 6-pounder quick-firing guns and several machine-guns; of the latter, only machine-guns.
The wheels at the rear were intended as steering aids, but their employment was abandoned after it was found that they easily became jammed or broken.

THE BATTLE OF FLERS-COURCELETTE

The objectives of the September offensive were the German Switch Line (a major obstacle covering High Wood and Martinpuich); high ground to the north-east of Combles; the German Third line at Flers; the fortified villages of Morval, Lesbœufs and Gueudecourt plus additional ground and defences in those vicinities. It was anticipated that a break of about three-and-a-half miles would occur in the enemy front facing Fourth Army. The Reserve Army, on the left, was to play a subsidiary role in which the Canadian Corps would take part. Cavalry was to exploit the expected breakthrough, with Bapaume being one of its goals.

Zero hour was fixed for 6.20 a.m. and hopes were held that all principal objectives would be taken by noon, after which Fourth Army was to begin 'rolling up' the German defences and advance northwards. Reliefs were carried out so that the assaulting troops would be fresh and fit for action.

Once more the stage was set for a major phase of the Somme offensive with, on the one hand, a confident Haig and subordinates and, on the other, a testing time for the recently appointed and successful team of Hindenburg and Ludendorff who, at the end of August, had taken over from the dismissed former Chief of the German General Staff, General Erich von Falkenhayn.

On the night of 13th September the tanks, which had come up by rail, began to move forward to their corps assembly places several miles away. As dusk came down next evening they once again ground their way towards the nearby front line with the aid of men with torches leading the way. Progress, however, was slow and difficult due to shell holes, mud, and mechanical trouble. Only 30, out of 42 originally earmarked for Fourth Army, eventually made it, plus another 6 for the Canadian Corps.

The secret had been well kept, and a feeling of potential victory was in the air as the hands of many watches moved towards zero hour.

Meantime, on the other side of No Man's Land, the unsuspecting Germans were about to receive one of the biggest surprises of the whole war, as they cowered beneath the British

Below: An aerial view of the terrain in front of Flers showing a sea of shell craters. It was across ground such as this that the newly arrived tanks had to struggle forward, and became fairly easy targets for enemy artillery.

Imperial War Museum

bombardment, the ferocity of which had been unequalled since 1st July. It had now gone on for three days and nights, pounding away at trenches, dug-outs and rear areas, with no let-up. Enemy batteries on the other hand, replied only fitfully and did not attempt to compete with the massed British artillery, even though it was obvious that an attack was due to take place.

During recent days, reports had, in fact, been received from forward observation balloons of a general build-up, and what appeared to be a new type of armoured car, behind the British lines; but no action had been taken by German Intelligence; and, as the noise of the tanks coming up to the front had been drowned by the barrage and the engines of aeroplanes detailed for that purpose, the enemy remained unaware of what was about to burst upon them.

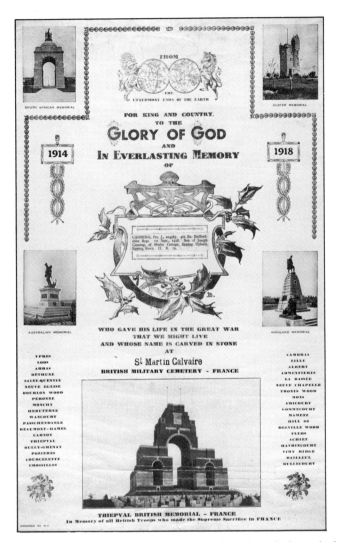

Above right: The tank memorial next to the site of the windmill at Pozières. It was erected to commemorate the first ever use of tanks, in the Battle of Flers-Courcelette, September 1916.

Below right: The Mark I Tank D17 at Flers, 17th September 1916. One of the four that assisted in the capture of Flers, it was hit by two shells and temporarily abandoned on the eastern side of the village. It was recovered later.

FLERS

It was the task of the 41st Division, in the centre of XV Corps, to capture this village and it was on this part of the front that the biggest concentration of tanks was made. To the left was the New Zealand Division and, on the right flank, the 14th.

Ten tanks were to operate towards and beyond Flers, with others (with the New Zealand Division) joining in as the battle progressed; but of the ten, only seven managed to reach the departure points.

A part of the Switch Line above Delville Wood was captured within the hour and Flers Trench, just south of the village, was taken half an hour later. Everything appeared to be going smoothly, and many of the enemy ran from the battlefield as they were confronted with the tanks, though here and elsewhere a number were hit by shell-fire and disabled. Nevertheless, four tanks pressed forward towards Flers, and one actually entered the village with cheering infantry behind it. The pilot of a British aircraft overhead witnessed it lurching up the main street with its machine-guns firing; and in due course his report was turned by the newspapers into an eye-witness account of a legendary feat of arms. Which it was, for on that day the tank in question (D16) helped to make history.

Three other tanks smashed into strongpoints and machine-gun nests along the eastern side of the village, and panic-stricken Germans fled from the ruins towards Gueudecourt. Isolated groups of enemy soldiers still held out bravely, but by 10 a.m. all resistance had ceased.

Above right: Ruins of Flers Church, 11th May 1917 with, in the foreground, the main street where Tank D16 helped to make history.

Below-right: A horse-drawn watercart plods along Flers main street past the rebuilt church, outside which stands a statue of a French soldier. At the end of the village is a 41st Division memorial, identical to the Royal Fusiliers memorial in Holborn, London. Surprisingly, there is no tank memorial in the village.

Imperial War Museum

By then, however, losses to our troops — particularly in officers — had been quite heavy; and the enemy had laid on a stiff bombardment. Even so, small groups of our men pushed on beyond Flers; but others, now that the initial excitement had died down, sought the shelter of captured trenches.

Any further ideas about renewing the attack that day were abandoned and this respite once again enabled the Germans to reinforce their front.

Whatever may be thought of Haig's insistence on the early use of the tanks, one indisputable fact remains; 15th September 1916 was a day of considerable historical importance. An entirely new weapon of warfare had been introduced, and one that was to have far-reaching influence on the strategy of later years.

Above: The Kaiser walking with Field-Marshal Hindenburg (left) and General Ludendorff at German G.H.Q. Spa, Belgium. Hindenburg succeeded General Falkenhayn as Chief of the General Staff on 29th August 1916, and Ludendorff became First Quarter-master General on the same date.

Above: The New Zealand Divison's memorial, north of Longueval and not far from Flers, unveiled in 1922. The division suffered almost 7,000 casualties between 15th September and 4th October 1916 when it was in constant action.

I have never seen anything quite so bad as the German front line on 15th September. The trench was full of dead, mostly apparently killed by concussion, and you could not move along the line without walking over the dead bodies. A British tank was ditched in the Jerry front trench.

I was one of the regimental stretcher-bearers at the time and I can distinctly remember the tank going through Flers and moving towards the village pump with a group of stretcher-bearers close behind it. Other soldiers were following and they certainly appeared to be happy although I cannot recall whether they were cheering. I was there all day, from the time we went over the top until about 5 p.m. I can remember Major Sadd standing at the starting tapes. He was killed at about 10a.m. that day. I understand that a shell fell close to where he was, in the lea of a trench, and both he and his servant were knocked out.

W. F. Chapman

MARTINPUICH

We made for the heap of debris and tottering walls that represented the village. This must have been Martinpuich. A long, steep street leading down-hill towards a main road. A terrible scene of desolation and destruction bore witness to the effectiveness of our ordnance. Dead men, looking like heaps of rags, were scattered here and there, some of them horribly mangled and torn, minus legs, arms and other parts of the body. Wrecked transport limbers and a line of slain and horribly swollen horses along the whole length of the village street. It looked as if on some recent night our gunners must have dropped their pills on some rationing convoy. Broken walls, heaps of bricks, smashed furniture and household articles lay strewn everywhere, pathetic lares et penates of French villagers, and now only fit for fuel purposes!

Giles Eyre

Imperial War Museum

Above right: The village church at Martinpuich, useful only as a makeshift shelter from high explosive.

Below right: The same place, fifty-five years later.

COURCELETTE

As part of the overall assault of 15th September, Courcelette was to be attacked by the Canadian Corps of the Reserve Army. The village and the ground beyond it, on which was situated the notorious 'Regina Trench', were to become to the Canadians what Pozières was to the Australians.

As at Flers, tanks made their début on this part of the front and the available half-dozen rumbled forward as the infantry jumped off. Three of the machines were directed to move along and each side of the main Bapaume road, and it is possible that this action was the reason for the tank memorial subsequently being situated opposite the site of the old windmill on that highway.

The Canadians overcame opposition at a strongpoint in a sugar factory, then swept on to Courcelette, and quickly captured the ruins of the village. But then they became involved in much bitter fighting, under extremely trying conditions, culminating in very heavy losses.

Imperial War Museum

Above right: Battle of Flers-Courcelette. Shells bursting in the village of Courcelette, September 1916. From the angle of this photograph it was most probably taken from just by the Albert — Bapaume road, the present site of a memorial erected by the Canadians.

Below right: Courcelette, July 1973, from the wall of the Canadian memorial by the side of the Bapaume road. In the far distance, to the right of, and above, the large house, is Regina Trench Military Cemetery.

If hell is as bad as what I have seen at Courcelette, I would not wish my worst enemy to go there.

A Canadian battalion commander

Above right: Courcelette after the Canadians had taken possession of it. The church is in the centre background, with just a stump of its original tower remaining.

Below right: Courcelette today. Not far away is Regina Trench Military Cemetery.

Above right: Courcelette, October 1916. The battlefield, with shells bursting in the distance and dead in the foreground.

Below right: Regina Trench Military Cemetery, July 1973, with Grandcourt beyond. The cemetery contains 2,265 graves and is situated a few hundred yards from the site of the trench. This ground was the scene of some of the most vicious fighting ever to have taken place during the Somme offensive.

In the words of the Canadian official historian, Colonel G. W. L. Nicholson: "Regina Trench, the capture of which had cost so much blood, was no longer a position of strength. Repeated bombardments had reduced it to a mere depression in the chalk, in many places blown twenty feet wide, and for long stretches almost filled with debris and dead bodies."

Canadian battle casualties at the Somme totalled 24,029, of which almost two thirds could be laid at the door of "that mere depression in the chalk."

Imperial War Museum

THE BATTLE OF MORVAL

When plans were first discussed for the September offensive Combles had been included by General Rawlinson as one of the main objectives. Amended plans allowed for the 'pinching out' of this village by joining up with our French Allies to the east of Morval which itself was due to be captured on the first day.

But things did not go according to plan, and it was not until 25th September that Morval and Lesbœufs fell, during what came to be known as the Battle of Morval. Subsidiary, but nevertheless vicious, fighting took place prior to these successes, during which the German second line strongpoint of Falfemont Farm was captured. Leuze Wood (known as 'Lousy Wood') also fell to the 5th Division, apart from the north-eastern corner.

Preliminary skirmishes towards Combles during the early days of September met with heavy machine-gun fire, particularly from a major enemy defensive position known as the Quadrilateral. Losses, as usual, were considerable and the amount of ground gained was limited.

The Battle of Morval officially opened on the 25th September with zero hour having been fixed at 12.35 p.m. to suit the French who were on the right of XIV Corps and in touch with the 56th Division. The capture of Combles was to be a combined effort on the 26th with the French attacking from the south. Two of our tanks were to be used. Meanwhile, other formations were involved further north with Morval and Lesbœufs as the objectives of XIV Corps and Gueudecourt (which tank D6 reached on September 15th before being destroyed) being the responsibility of XV Corps. Cavalry was once more ordered to stand by.

A fierce creeping barrage preceeded the assaulting troops as they jumped off, and for once casualties were less heavy than normal — possibly due, in part, to the excellent co-operation of our artillery. On their part of the front men of the Guards Division stormed in with the bayonet and considerable slaughter resulted from this encounter in the confines of the enemy trenches. On their right the 5th, 6th and 56th Divisions also swept forward and did deadly execution to the enemy, with the first objective soon

being taken. Morval fell to the 95th Brigade of 5th Division while the southern part of Lesbœufs was cleared by the 1st West Yorks of 18th Brigade. The remainder of that village was secured by the Guards. Following these captures, the Germans commenced a heavy bombardment which did little more than reduce the ruins to finer rubble and dust.

At Gueudecourt, however, the 21st Divison found itself in difficulties due to heavy machine-gun fire. On the following day a tank turned an important enemy trench into an abattoir with the aid of a low flying British aircraft which machine-gunned the defenders. Later cavalry entered the village and even patrolled beyond. By evening troops of the 110th Brigade had dug in at the far end of the ruins of Gueudecourt.

Late on the night of the 25th September orders were issued by Fourth Army headquarters for Combles to be surrounded on

Imperial War Museum

Above: Battle of Morval. Waves of infantry moving forward and passing one of the Mark 1 tanks detailed to work with the Fourth Army but which became ditched soon after zero hour, near Ginchy, 25th September 1916.

the morrow in co-operation with the French. Just previous to this however, a report had been received that it was the intention of the enemy to evacuate the village during that very night; and prompt action was taken by the 56th Division to probe forward. Patrols reconnoitred the outskirts; and in the early hours of the morning, contact was made in and around the village with the French. The latter had encountered some slight opposition, but the enemy had, in fact, mainly departed towards other defensive positions.

Much booty was found in Combles, mostly by the French, and this included a considerable amount of ammunition and rifles. Five hundred prisoners were also taken.

Further limited fighting along the front followed during the next couple of days but on the 28th September, and in accordance with an earlier request by General Foch, part of the line then held by the 20th and 56th Divisions of XIV Corps was handed over to the French. Morval and Lesbœufs then came under their control to enable them more room for manoeuvre and the Battle of Morval came to an end.

BATTLE OF MORVAL

Above left: All that remained of the church at Lesbœufs ten months after the fighting — a mound of bricks and a bell.

Below left: A grave in a shell hole near Combles, apparently of 'Pte P. Lynch'.

Above right: The entrance to the Catacombs, Combles, next to the church and surrounded by ruins of the village, 2nd January 1917.
The Catacombs were large underground caverns and passages used as shelters and also for storage purposes.

Below right: The Square in front of the church, Combles, July 1971, with a sign to the Guards' Cemetery.

Imperial War Museum

The view through the broken windows showed the square utterly deserted, and ploughed up by the shells, which had strewn it with the branches of the limes. The artillery fire that raged round the place without ceasing deepened the gloom of this appalling picture. Now and then the gigantic crash of a 38-centimetre shell dominated the tumult; whereupon a hail of splinters swept through Combles, clattering through the branches of the trees, or striking on the walls of the few houses that were still left standing, and bringing down the slates from the roofs.

In the course of the afternoon the firing increased to such a degree that single explosions were no longer audible. There was nothing but one terrific tornado of noise. From 7 onwards the square and the houses around were shelled at intervals of half a minute with 15-centimetre shells. There were many duds among them, which all the same made the house rock.

Ernst Junger

After breakfast I went out to have a look round. Heavy artillery had turned a peaceful little billeting town into a scene of desolation in the course of a day or two. Whole houses had been flattened by single direct hits or blown up so that the interiors of the rooms hung over the chaos like the scenes on a stage. A sickly scent of dead bodies rose from many of the ruins, for many civilians had been caught in the bombardment and buried beneath the wreckage of their homes. A little girl lay dead in a pool of blood on the threshold of one of the doorways.

Ernst Junger

Wheel spoke from German supply limber found in a newly dug ditch.

British artilleryman's spur found by the author.

Above left: Main street, Combles, September 1916.

Below left: and in July 1971.

THIEPVAL FALLS AT LAST

In spite of all the previous set-backs Sir Douglas Haig was still determined to continue his pressure on the Germans who, he was convinced, were reaching a point where their reserves would soon be exhausted.

His next aim was to clear the Thiepval Ridge on which sporadic but tough fighting had carried on since the capture of Pozieres. Also in his mind was the possibility of additional operations, including an assault on Gommecourt by Third Army.

The main attack was to encompass the ground from Courcelette to — and including — the Schwaben Redoubt, with the assault being delivered by two divisions of the Canadian Corps under Lieut.-Gen. Hon. Sir J. H. G. Byng, and two divisions of II Corps commanded by Lieut.-Gen. C. W. Jacob. Zero hour was 12.35 p.m. on the 26th September.

The village of Thiepval, surmounting the immense fortress which had been the scene of a bloody repulse on 1st July, was by now nothing more than a ruin. However, its massive, deep shelters were mostly intact, and it still presented a formidable obstacle. For this reason six of the eight tanks available for the overall assault were allotted to II Corps.

It was also necessary to capture Mouquet Farm which had defied constant attacks by British, Australian and Canadian troops. Bitter fighting had taken place in and around the heap of rubble which was all that was left of this farm; but each time the enemy had managed to cling on to the numerous underground tunnels and dug-outs beneath and had emerged time and time again behind our troops, to attack them from the rear. It was a position of much importance, he had every intention of retaining it, and fought savagely to do so.

At zero hour the Canadians on the right flank dashed forward and one battalion quickly reached the enemy front line. Because of serious casualties some units were not so fortunate, and yet another was forced to remain in its trenches under heavy shell-fire. Other Canadians moved towards Regina Trench and all along their front severe fighting developed, with losses being caused by

. . . The salient made by our advance into the enemy line was very noticeable. It encircled Thiepval, starting from Leipzig Salient, a small corner of the German position south of Thiepval, which was the only position of the enemy line that the Fourth Army had managed to seize on the left of their attack during the first day of the battle.

In that Salient, Mouquet Farm became the centre of German resistance. It was prominently situated half-way up a long slope, with Thiepval higher up and several strong redoubts, of which Schwaben was one, above and below. If the enemy was driven out he would have to straighten up his line and give up a good deal of ground. He had made use of the dry chalky soil by constructing deep dug-outs and tunnels, which securely sheltered his reserves. Day and night shells of every calibre unceasingly blew up the place. Every one of our attacks met with a stiff resistance.

Paul Maze

Above: Mouquet (Mucky) Farm, showing clearly the powerful German trench system surrounding the farm buildings, which had also been fortified. This picture was taken before the Somme offensive got under way; later, all the ground seen here became a moonscape of craters, with the remains of the farm indistinguishable from the torn-up terrain.

enfilading machine-gun fire. Nevertheless, at the end of the day the results of the operations were considered by the Canadian Corps to have been satisfactory.

Fierce clashes also occurred on the left of the Canadians around Zollern Redoubt, Stuff Redoubt and Mouquet Farm, with heavy losses being inflicted on troops of the British 11th Division. Confused fighting took place amongst the rubble of the farm itself and two tanks became ditched before they were able to be of assistance. The crew of one however, used its machine-guns to advantage. Men of the Lancashire Fusiliers, 11th Manchesters and 5th Dorsets were all involved in the struggle and they were later joined by a detachment of the 6th East Yorkshire Pioneers. Eventually, after smoke bombs had been thrown into the cellar entrances the survivors of the German garrison, amounting to one officer and fifty-five other ranks surrendered.

Further to the left other strongpoints and trenches were attacked successfully by the 18th Division and, although heavy machine-gun fire was encounted, losses were less than in other areas. A tank — which became ditched shortly afterwards — had a hand in persuading groups of Germans to surrender near Thiepval. Shortly afterwards heavy fire from the ruined village held up the advance on the front of the 53rd Brigade.

It was to the 54th Brigade that one of the most difficult tasks had been given. This was the capture of the western part of Thiepval and then the Schwaben Redoubt, almost half-a-mile beyond the village. Two tanks were to assist in the operation.

At first all went well but heavy machine-gun fire sweeping the slopes from the ruins of the chateau — just as it had done nearly three months before — caused a serious problem. On this occasion however, one of the tanks arrived and crushed all

Above left: Mouquet Farm battlefield, October 1916. The farm was not captured until 26th September, yet it was originally an objective for the 11th Sherwood Foresters on 1st July!

Below left: The farm itself is back to normal, though traces of trenches can still be seen in the area today. The quarry (in foreground, surrounded by trees) was an important feature during the battle.

Imperial War Museum

resistance. Then it too became ditched; it had proved its worth, but being disabled, left the issue still in doubt.

The advance continued slowly with many skirmishes taking place and eventually most of the village was in our hands except for the north-western corner and some trenches.

Early next morning fresh attempts were made all along the front; but resistance was strong. Bitter fighting continued over the next few days, with the losses mounting and rain and mud adding to the difficulties of the troops. The remainder of Thiepval finally passed into our hands; but Stuff Redoubt and Schwaben Redoubt proved to be powerful obstacles with terrible struggles taking place, including hand-to-hand fighting in and around trenches and shell-holes that were deep in mud. Similar conditions applied on the right where the Canadians doggedly fought on towards their goal at a heavy cost in lives.

September came to a close with the protagonists of both sides in a state of near exhaustion.

As October opened, more rain fell and conditions worsened. Further attempts on Regina Trench claimed more Canadian victims and during the night of 3rd October the 2nd Canadian Division was relieved after having suffered more than 6,500 casualties. Its place was taken by the 3rd Canadian Division, with the 1st Canadian Division taking over the right of the corps twenty-four hours later. On II Corps front the 11th Divison was relieved by the 25th Division after having incurred more than 5,000 casualties. The 18th Divison came out of the line with over 3,300 losses.

On the 9th October Stuff Redoubt fell to troops of the 25th Divison, and in spite of constant counter-attacks, remained in the hands of 7th Brigade who, a few days later, were dug in on ground overlooking Grandcourt.

Above left: The ruins of Thiepval village from the British front line, September 1916. The scene of terrible carnage on 1st July, the village was finally cleared of the enemy on 27th September.

Below left: Thiepval 1971; traces of old trenches still remained on these slopes at that time.

On the 14th the honour of driving the Germans from their last hold on the Schwaben Redoubt fell to the 39th Division which had taken over from the 18th Division. Severe fighting continued until very late that night, and in spite of fierce but unsuccessful counter-attacks next day — during which flame throwers were used by the enemy — this former bastion of the German defence system became incorporated into our front.

At last the massive fortress of Thiepval, with its powerful flank defences, had fallen — 3½ months after our troops had first been hurled against it.

Below: Mill Road Military Cemetery, on the crown of the former Schwaben Redoubt, from the Ulster Tower.

THE CONCLUDING WEEKS

Following the fall of Thiepval Sir Douglas Haig decided to allow the enemy no respite and contemplated a continuation of the advance over a wide front in which the Fourth Army, Reserve Army and Third Army were to make a combined effort.

However, the weather then took a hand; rain, mist and mud forced major revisions of the original plan, with the fighting once again relapsing into more localised — but nevertheless savage — actions. The New Zealand Division of XV Corps and the Canadians played important roles in these new attacks, while numerous British formations were also hurled against the German defences.

These operations, which became known as the Battle of the Transloy Ridges and the Battle of the Ancre Heights, took place in rapidly deteriorating conditions which caused rifles and machine-guns to become clogged with mud. One of the earlier results of these engagements was the capture, by the 23rd Division, of Le Sars, which was close to the infamous Butte de Warlincourt from which the enemy was able to observe all movement within our lines. It was near here that South African troops were hard hit by machine-gun fire as they battled their way forward. Regina Trench also was again the scene of desperate fighting as the Canadians endeavoured to capture this strong and bitterly contested enemy defensive position. After sustaining almost 3,000 casualties the Canadian 3rd Division was taken out of the line, and the 4th Canadian Division took their place. Later, when the remainder of the Canadian Corps was relieved, this Division came under the jurisdiction of II Corps.

By mid-October conditions all along the main battle front were shocking, with deep mud, water, rain and mist making or-dinary existence a severe trial to the soldiers of both sides. Shell-bursts were smothered by the ooze, artillery positions and dug-outs were flooded, and it became increasing difficult to move troops, guns and transport. In spite of this, General Joffre, the French Commander-in-Chief, pressed General Haig to resume the offensive, and in consequence met with a rebuff from the British military leader.

The bad weather did not let-up until the beginning of November, and then only for a short period after which it once more clamped down, and the troops suffered accordingly. Meanwhile, fighting continued with modified plans taking the place of earlier, more ambitious, objectives. Most of Regina Trench finally passed into our hands following an attack on 21st October by II Corps, in which the 39th, 25th, 18th (British) and 4th (Canadian) divisions were heavily engaged. Stuff Trench, another enemy strongpoint, fell at the same time.

Imperial War Museum

Above: THE EYES OF THE GUNS. The Somme offensive was primarily an infantry 'show' but it should not be forgotten that other arms of the services gave important support during the course of the struggle. Much good work was done by the R.F.C. in flimsy aircraft such as the BE2c seen above flying close to a derelict mill. Although slow and cum-bersome they were usefully employed for artillery observation and photographic duties.

The immortal Albert Ball flew on the Somme front, and another famous British airman in that sector was Major L. G. Hawker V. C. The latter met his death in November 1916 from the guns of Baron Manfred von Richthofen (The Red Knight), who was just beginning his rise to fame at that time.

It was not until the 10th November that the weather allowed another attempt to be made on that portion of Regina Trench still in enemy hands. On that night the Canadians assaulted in the light of the moon and within a short time they were amongst the Germans with practically all that hated trench then coming into our possession.

Additional attempts were made to push forward to Le Transloy but the dreadful condition of the ground, where in places men were up to their waists in mud and slime, frustrated all drives in that direction. Attacks were also made with a view to capturing the Butte de Warlencourt but these too fizzled out in the appalling mud, although initially men of the Durhams fought their way on to the Butte itself. In pouring rain, troops of the Anzac Corps attacked a German salient north of Gueudecourt, but failed to obtain their objective after struggling over the water-logged terrain.

On the right the French were also in trouble due to the weather; and subsequently Gen. Foch gave up all ideas of major attacks. Except at one or two places our Allies concentrated their activities in consolidating the line they already held.

Imperial War Museum

Gas shells exploding near the Canadian lines, October 1916. It is not difficult to visualize the state of this ground in bad weather, or the conditions under which the men fought.

British .303 SMLE rifle still retaining vestiges of its wooden stock.

THE BATTLE OF THE ANCRE

The final phase of the Somme offensive covered the period between the 13th and 19th November 1916, after which the battle came to an end in a morass of mud with the combatants utterly exhausted and thoroughly bogged down. It did not, however, mean a complete end to the fighting which flared up every so often, mainly as a result of General Haig's insistence on the enemy being continually harrassed "by every possible means" including trench raids and other aggressive acts.

Prior to that stage being reached General Gough, at Fifth Army headquarters, had deliberated on the weather situation and general ground conditions, and decided to press home another attack on V Corps front, to begin at 5.45 a.m. on the 13th November. The initial objective — far less ambitious than previous plans — was to 'take out' the pronounced bulge, or salient, in the line. This would necessitate the capture of Beaucourt, including the station, Beaumont Hamel, the Redan Ridge and Serre. All these places were original goals on 1st July, four-and-a-half months earlier. Pys and Irles were given as additional tasks in the event of the main assault being successful. The use of tanks had been envisaged in the plan but because of the unsatisfactory ground conditions the actual number that took part in the attack was small. As it happened most of those that did participate became stuck in the mud.

The assault commenced over a depressing and dripping battlefield that was shrouded in fog. Nevertheless this effectively covered the movement of our troops who burst upon the surprised Germans with, on the right, St. Pierre Divion quickly falling to men of the 39th Division. Across the Ancre units of the 63rd (R.N.) Division battered their way into the German front line — although at a heavy cost in casualties due to machine-gun fire — and then captured Beaucourt Station. To their left the 51st Division started forward to the roar of a mine blown at Hawthorn Crater (scene of the controversial mine explosion of 1st July) and although a hold-up occurred at 'Y Ravine', Beaumont Hamel was entered early in the afternoon with Scottish formations well to the

Below: German barbed wire entanglements in the Beaumont Hamel area, November 1916. This is what ordinary men of flesh and blood had to contend with in those grim days.

Imperial War Museum

115

fore. By late afternoon the ruins of that village — once believed by the Germans to be impregnable — were behind our troops and the debacle of 1st July was avenged. The 2nd Division attacked along the Redan Ridge but came up against heavy machine-gun fire which caused serious losses. Intact German wire, mud and fog all added to the confusion and the attackers, who had at first met with partial success, had to pull back from their forward gains.

On the front of 3rd Division, by Serre, the fog was not so thick but the condition of the ground was appalling. In many instances the attackers were waist deep in mud and water and, even though they struggled forward under heavy fire, it was found that the German wire was still mostly intact. In spite of these terrible obstacles groups of men thrust their way into the German trenches where bitter fighting took place. Eventually these gallant bands were overwhelmed as heavy artillery fire prevented a back-up attack being delivered.

To the north of Serre two Yorkshire battalions of the 31st Division (XIII Corps) had also attacked with vigour but there too the story was somewhat similar — success at first, to be followed later by retirement after serious losses had been incurred due to strong German counter-attacks and heavy enemy shell-fire.

Thus at the end of the day the tiny village of Serre, which had been the scene of awful slaughter on 1st July, was still in the hands of the enemy. It was destined to remain so until he voluntarily withdrew during the Retreat to the Hindenburg Line.

V Corps continued the assault next morning and Beaucourt fell to troops led by Lieut.-Col. B. C. Freyberg (in the course of time to become Lord Freyberg) who had already been wounded. During the day he received a further severe wound from a shell and was carried back from the line. Later he was awarded the V.C. for his magnificent leadership.

During the next few days further bitter and confused fighting took place as our men slowly tried to push their way forward in the mud. General Haig expressed doubts on the logic of continuing the offensive but General Gough was keen to keep trying. In fact he had stipulated that Grandcourt should be an additional objective (to be taken by II Corps) but this attempt was finally

Above: The 51st (Highland) Division memorial, surmounting the old German front line trenches in the Newfoundland Memorial Park, Beaumont Hamel, July 1973. The Highlander faces Beaumont Hamel, and is a few yards from the notorious 'Y Ravine', captured by this division on 13th November 1916 — more than four months after the original disastrous attempt by the Newfoundlanders and the 1st Essex.

Imperial War Museum

dropped when the weather, which for a short time had cleared, clamped down again and the first snow of winter fell.

Nevertheless, in the most shocking conditions of blinding sleet and rain, with visibility being virtually nil, Canadian troops floundered forward beyond Regina Trench in the early morning light of 18th November. On their left, men of the 18th Division also attacked but came under deadly machine-gun fire with heavy losses. A similar situation prevailed with the 19th Division, although the south-western end of Grandcourt was entered by the 8th Gloucesters. Other men from the 56th Brigade joined up with them later but during the night of 19th November they were withdrawn to a position further back.

On the left Serre was once more entered, this time by troops of the 14th Brigade, but yet again the survivors were overwhelmed by enemy counter-attacks.

It had now become clear that any further possibility of renewing the assault was out of the question for, with rain pouring down on the mud-covered battlefield and with the troops exhausted and soaked to the skin, relief of the tired divisions became imperative.

Above left: 'Beaumont Hamel must have been a very pretty spot before the war' (W. J. Bradley)

Below left: It was: and it is now.

The Autumn attacks had been a sprawling muddle of attrition and inconclusiveness. In the early summer the Fourth Army had been ready to advance with a new impetus. Now it was stuck in the frozen mud in front of Bapaume, like a derelict tank. And the story was the same all the way up to Ypres. Bellicose politicians and journalists were fond of using the word 'crusade'. But the 'chivalry' (which I'd seen in epitome at the Army School) had been mown down and blown up in July, August, and September, and its remnant had finished the year's 'crusade' in a morass of torment and frustration.

Siegfried Sassoon

117

MUDDY MISERY

Typical examples of the awful swamp-like conditions of the Somme battlefields with (left) transport horses and wagons in difficulties; (below left) sleds used for transporting wounded, Le Sars, and (below right) British troops coming out of the trenches at Guillemont.

The photographs were taken in July, October and November respectively, and emphasise one of the major problems confronting men and animals all through the offensive.

Stumbling across miles of old battlefield, first through horse-lines and dumps, then through dreary wastes of clay pitted with shell-holes full of mud, strewn with the litter of old equipment and shell-splinters, and smelling vilely of old corpses, one came to a wide swampy valley. Down in the bottom, in the central middle distance, there rose out of the mud a strange conical mound of white chalk, a hundred feet high. It was known as the Butte of Warlencourt and marked the German front line. While the artillery of both armies lay back on the hill-tops strafing anyone who moved by day down the long slopes to the Butte, the infantry crouched and hid in the mud of the valley bottom. Even by night one could scarcely move for the enemy spasmodically plastered with shell-fire every line of approach. To go or come from the line was a nightmare adventure and once there, one dared not move for fear of the enemy machine-guns on the Butte of Warlencourt. That ghastly hill, never free from the smoke of bursting shells, became fabulous. It shone white in the night and seemed to leer at you like an ogre in a fairy tale. It loomed up unexpectantly, peering into trenches where you thought you were safe: it haunted your dreams. Twenty-four hours in the trenches before the Butte finished a man off.

C. E. Carrington (Charles Edmunds)

Below: CHECKPOINT. Where the Somme offensive bogged down in the appalling mud of the area bisected by the Bapaume road, seen here stretching into the distance. The town — Fourth Army's original objective — lies less than four miles away. On the left can be seen part of the ruins of Le Sars, and over to the right, in the valley, is the hump of the hated Butte de Warlencourt.

This picture was taken in 1919, when the hand of nature was already beginning to hide the ravages of war.

TO SUM UP

Thus the Somme offensive ground to a standstill nearly five months after it had started. The high hopes of July, immediately quenched, finally drowned in the November mud.

Haig had fulfilled his promise to help the French, and we had paid heavily for it; whether he was right to pursue the offensive after the situation at Verdun had eased and the casualty lists had become so swollen, remains arguable. He believed he was right, so did the French, and so do many still. What is not arguable is that at times the strategy was at fault, and too much was expected of insufficiently trained troops.

To most people, the Somme offensive seems a ghastly failure and a criminal waste of lives. And yet, on the Somme, the illusion of German invincibility was shattered. Both Hindenburg and Ludendorff knew that the German Army could not afford a second such battle; it had been fought to a standstill.

In spite of this, the German Army remained a force to be reckoned with for over two more years, and — this was the greatest tragedy of the whole bloody, drawn-out affair — all the ground won at such a terrible cost changed hands again within a very short period during the German 'push' of 1918.

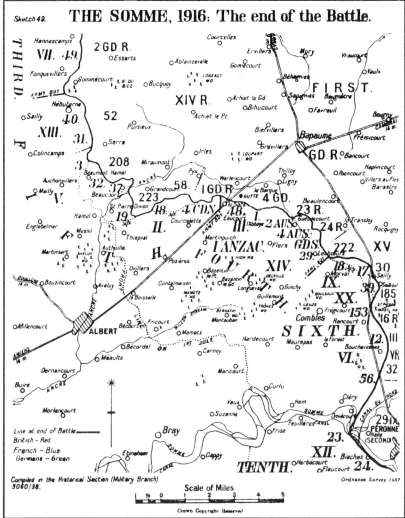

Left: On the Somme its past is never far away. This was an ordinary picnic, but it was on the site of the old German line at Serre; only when it was set out did the author notice the shell lying behind the tree.

THE PRICE OF VALOUR
TOTAL CASUALTIES OF THE SOMME OFFENSIVE

It is impossible to arrive at a final figure for casualties. Sir Charles Oman, who investigated enemy casualty lists, came to the conclusion that losses on both sides had been 'about exactly the same', i.e. 560,000. In 1932, and compiled on a different data basis, this figure was amended by the Official Historian, Brig.-Gen. Sir James E. Edmunds, who calculated that the losses were 'around 600,000, the French and British slightly over that figure, and the Germans slightly under it'.

Further adjustments were made later when the German Official History became available, but as it was not very specific on Somme casualties, a certain amount of guesswork remained necessary. The Germans admitted to at least 500,000, but apparently did not include any estimate of those slightly wounded, missing, taken prisoner, or even the victims of the original bombardment. In consequence, the total must have been proportionately greater.

The British always included the latter categories in their casualty lists; and the evidence from published figures indicates that the Germans suffered greater losses than the British (419,654) and French (204,253) combined.

53 British divisions were involved in the fighting, four of them Canadian, four Australian and one New Zealand. The French ultimately put into the field a total of 20 divisions. The Germans, on the other hand, used up the strength of 95½ divisions, of which 43½ were employed twice, and four as much as three times.

Not a road, not a track, not a copse, not a tree, not a brick does not possess its scar of tragedy, nor yet its halo of heroism.

Graham Seton Hutchison

A DEATH IN HOSPITAL

Dear Heart, how longingly, I thought of thee,
When nurses tip-toed round that bed, red-eyed,
And stole away to hide their sobbing in the corridors,
Afraid that even that pale face should stir to sound,
Wrapped in the last great calm that only is angelic —
Then from the bed, a rasp of breath in long intake and shuddering fall!

We held our hearts, we who had life to live,
And thought our thoughts, but said nothing
Of that deep fear which stirs the soul of man
When brothers go from them and give from dust
A new-won soul within the hand of God.

Then, at the close a whisper — that was all —
We knew that one brave heart had ceased,
And, with an agony subdued but passionately sad, a woman's sobbing!
Our eyes were wet, we could not think
But of ourselves were our dear ones to weep in vain for us —

Hugh Quigley

The King and the Prince of Wales at a soldier's grave in 1916.

THE DEAD

These hearts were woven of human joys and cares,
Washed marvellously with sorrow, swift to mirth.
The years had given them kindness. Dawn was theirs,
And sunset, and the colours of the earth.
These had seen movement, and heard music; known
Slumber and waking; loved; gone proudly friended;
Felt the quick stir of wonder; sat alone;
Touched flowers and furs and cheeks. All this is ended.

Rupert Brooke

PART 3

WINTER OF DISCONTENT

The abandonment of the Somme offensive certainly did not mean an end to the miseries of the troops. The advent of winter vastly increased the discomfort of the men as they floundered in seas of mud or tried to exist in waterlogged rat-infested trenches, with little cover from the incessant rain, intense cold and enemy machine-guns.

Parapets collapsed, dug-outs filled with water, trenches became quagmires and everywhere gloom settled over the soaked battlefield. Guns could not be moved without considerable effort with additional teams of horses, food and water had to be carried for long distances on duckboard tracks that continually sank beneath the mud, and exhaustion and sickness became rampant. Men and animals drowned in the mud, and, as the weather worsened, frostbite claimed numerous victims.

At the same time, a policy of aggressiveness was demanded by the military authorities who, in the comfort of their head-quarters at the rear, were quite unaware of the awful conditions in the battle areas. Orders were given for lines to be straightened in local attacks, raids were to be carried out and the enemy allowed no peace.

It is clear from the writings of those who actually fought at that time, that the morale of our troops was very low, and politicians, war correspondents and generals were all held in contempt. Anyone with red tabs became a focal point of near hatred. And yet, in spite of all, the comradeship and discipline, and the British sense of humour, of the front-line soldier still held him in good stead.

On the 27th December 1916, General Sir Douglas Haig was raised to the rank of Field-Marshal by H.M. the King. A few days later instructions were issued from his headquarters that limited operations were to be continued with the object of inducing the enemy to believe that the Battle of the Somme was recommencing.

Thus the casualty lists grew longer and the suffering continued.

Imperial War Museum

Above: Switch Trench, December 1916.

Opposite: Away in the distance near Albert a British stores dump burns to prevent it falling into German hands. It is March 1918 — the town was lost on the 27th.

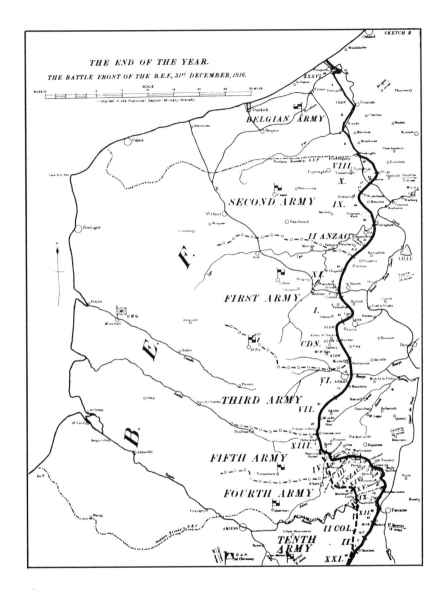

THE END OF THE YEAR.

THE BATTLE FRONT OF THE B.E.F., 31ST DECEMBER, 1916.

Imperial War Museum

Above: View of the snow covered battlefield at Pozières, February 1917. This picture was taken from near the orchard, north-west of the village, which was captured by the 8th Australian Battalion on 24th July 1916.

The map on the left shows, at the bottom, the area of ground captured from the enemy during the Somme offensive of 1916 in relation to the rest of the Western Front. It cost the three main combatants over 1,200,000 casualties.

THE GERMAN RETREAT TO THE HINDENBURG LINE

As long ago as the end of October 1916 British airmen had noticed fresh earthworks just over 14 miles east of the front line at Monchy au Bois, but it was not until the German retreat had actually started, on 24th February, that the new and powerful defence system opposite the British sector was plotted in full. On that day the first specific signs of a withdrawal appeared.

Although the British troops were at first delighted at the thought of a German retreat taking place, they were to find that it was not just a question of following up a defeated army, for the Germans left behind strong rearguards who took a heavy toll of any over-enthusiastic advancing troops.

Nevertheless, Serre and Pys were entered on the morning of 25th February; most of Pusieux was taken after stiff hand-to-hand fighting on the night of 26th February; and the remainder on the 27th. Gommecourt was found to be empty and was occupied by British troops. On 10th March fires were seen burning in villages east and south-east of Bapaume, and this, together with reports from prisoners, indicated that a general withdrawal to the Hindenburg Line was about to take place.

The retreat got under way in the middle of March. The Germans, however, were determined that the Allies should derive as little benefit as possible from it; buildings were blown up, railways and bridges destroyed, roads cratered, trees cut down, wells filled in or polluted, orchards up-rooted and civilians and animals removed to the rear. Booby traps were planted everywhere.

Above right: Remains of former homes in Serre, March 1917, after the Germans had left. It was to fall into their hands again a year later.

Below right: A British soldier sitting on a mound of bricks that was once Gommecourt church, after the Germans had voluntarily relinquished their hold on this fortress village in February 1917. The mass of barbed wire around the base of the former church typifies the strong defences of the area.

Imperial War Museum

Imperial War Museum

125

All along the line as they advanced, the British came up against stiffening resistance from enemy-occupied 'outpost' villages in front of the Hindenburg Line. Some fierce fighting ensued before those barriers were overcome, but by 8th April our men were mainly entrenched in front of the Hindenburg Line itself.

To the Allies, who had advanced more than ten miles at some points, it seemed a great victory which fully justified the bitter battles of the previous months; to the Germans, on the other hand, it was a sensible method of shortening their line and conserving troops.

Imperial War Museum

Above right: German Retreat to the Hindenburg Line. Transport of the 2nd Australian Division returning along the Bapaume road, March 1917. Le Sars railway station, The Quarry and the Butte de Warlencourt are in the background.

Below right: The same area in July 1973, with the Butte de Warlencourt covered in bushes and trees and looking like just a minor rise in the ground. On the Butte itself many shell holes can still be seen.

Above: Troops of the 8th Australian Infantry Brigade on the outskirts of Bapaume on the day the town was entered, 17th March 1917. Their exhaustion and their mud-covered clothes and equipment tell the story.

Above right: Australian troops of the 1st Anzac Corps in front of the Hotel de Ville in the Grande Place, Bapaume, 19th March 1917.
A few hours after this photograph was taken the Town Hall blew up, killing a number of Australians and two French Deputies; the Germans had booby-trapped it.

Below right: As it is now.

Plaque and commemorative scroll presented to the next-of-kin of those killed in the Great War, together with 1914-15 Star, British War Medal, and Victory Medal, known collectively by the British soldier as 'Pip, Squeak and Wilfred'. The faded snapshot tells its own story — the two brothers on the left were both killed in action.

Above right: Inhabitants of the village of Mons-en-Chaussée, which is on the Amiens-St. Quentin road south-east of Péronne, talking to British officers by the badly damaged church, after the Germans had pulled out. These people are actually standing on the edge of an enormous mine crater blown by the enemy to impede the British advance.

Below right: Picture taken in 1974 just a few yards from where the above meeting took place. The minor road on the left leads to the village of Athies where another vast mine was exploded in March 1917.

Above: Grande Place, Péronne, March 1917. The notice board on the Hotel de Ville reads 'Nicht argen, nur wundern!' A general translation of this is 'Don't be angry, just wonder.'

Right: The Grande Place, July 1973.

Above left: A view towards mist-shrouded St. Quentin from the British front line close to the Amiens road, 24th April 1917. The Hindenburg Line ran two miles west of St. Quentin, which was not entered by the Allies until 1st October 1918. This is where the retreat ended.

Below left: St Quentin in the distance, July 1973, from what is believed to be the exact spot as the one above. The author traced the war-time position from a trench map.

THE INTERLUDE

As our troops settled in before the vast fortifications of the Hindenburg Line, the tide of war moved from the Somme to other areas of the long battle front, and for almost a year comparative quiet reigned.

On 6th April 1917 America entered the war; but she was totally unprepared, and it was not until late in 1918 that the presence of her troops was really felt. Nevertheless she represented a serious threat to the enemy; and the German leaders obviously considered it better to act while there was still a chance of defeating the British and the French in the field. Russia's collapse in 1917 helped them to pursue that aim.

Above: A British 18-pdr battery caught by shell fire on a corduroy road, Lesbœufs, March 1918.

1918 — THE GERMAN 'PUSH' (OPERATION MICHAEL)

The blow fell on 21st March 1918. It was aimed at the thinly-held and extended front of General Gough's Fifth Army, still recuperating from the mauling it had received during 'Third Ypres'. Three German armies attacked simultaneously in that sector, and against half of the front held by General Byng's Third Army, on Gough's left flank.

After an overwhelming barrage from more than 6,000 guns, masses of elite, highly trained German storm troops swept forward in thick mist. Utter confusion reigned in the British lines as many units that had survived the terrifying bombardment (which had included gas) were cut off and destroyed. Due to his man-power problem — he had a front of 42 miles to cover with only twelve infantry divisions and three cavalry divisions — General Gough had decided to rely on powerful strongpoints defended by numerous machine-guns. But the fog enabled the enemy to by-pass many of these defensive positions, and as the day wore on things became desperate.

General Ludendorff's strategy was aimed at separating the British and French Armies, with the object of driving the former back to the sea, before turning on the French in the hope that they would sue for peace.

Withdrawals began on the Fifth Army front, and on the second day the British Third positions fell to the enemy in the south. Within 48 hours the battle raged in the open, with over 60 German divisions being engaged.

Péronne was abandoned on 23rd March, and the retreat continued towards the old Somme battlefields. On 25th March the Germans attacked violently all along the front, and, in the south, forced back the British from positions they were holding on the Somme Canal. By the same evening the enemy had driven a deep wedge across the old battlefield zone and had reached the Ancre near Beaumont Hamel. Bapaume, Maricourt, and other towns and villages — many of them in flames — were all captured.

Albert fell to the Germans and a new line was established just west of the town; Amiens, too, was under fire. Scratch units were hurriedly got together in some places, and men who had never thought that they would be engaged in fighting found themselves charging towards the Germans with fixed bayonets. Batmen, cooks, drivers and other non-combatants, all played their part and helped to repulse the enemy.

The date of 28th March had been chosen by the Germans to mount a major attack on the Third Army front at Arras. Seven divisions were thrown against four British; but this time they met with a bloody repulse, and the assault ended in failure.

On 4th April a further massive attack was mounted against British units who were then holding the line outside Villers-Bretonneux. Heavy blows fell elsewhere along the line, but, apart from limited enemy successes, the offensive began to run out of steam. There was one further attack on Villers-Bretonneux on 24th April where, for a time, the town was in the hands of the enemy. In this last real attempt to break through to Amiens, less than 11 miles away, the Germans were supported by thirteen tanks, for the first time. The British brought up thirteen Mark IVs and several 'Whippets', and the first-ever tank battle took place.

By noon on the 25th the town was reoccupied, and a further planned German attack was abandoned. After this latest failure to smash through to Amiens, the enemy gave up his main efforts on that front, although fighting did not die down completely for some weeks.

So ended the German 'push' on the Somme front. It came very close to success, and had the gamble come off, the course of the war would have been very different. It was a costly offensive for all concerned, the British incurring over 170,000 casualties, the French 77,000, and the Germans about the same number as the overall total of the Allies.

Footnote: 'Whippets' were light tanks with a crew of three, and were armed with 4 Hotchkiss machine-guns. They were capable of achieving a speed of 8-9 m.p.h.'.

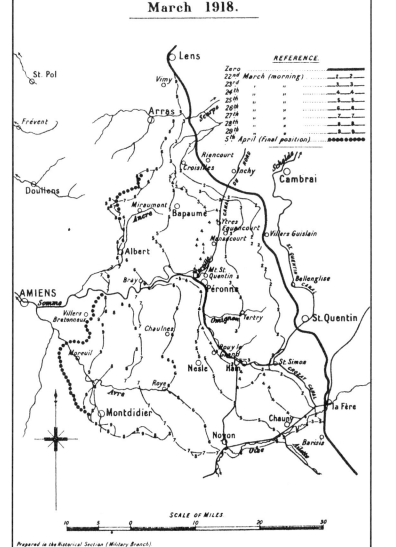

Imperial War Museum

Above: Four British soldiers lying dead outside a dug-out in the Somme fighting zone during the German spring offensive.

Above left: Villers-Bretonneux, with the ruined church in the centre, from the German trenches. The town, which was of strategic importance, was taken by the enemy on 24th April 1918, but was recaptured next day after bitter night fighting. It was here that the Australians, in particular, won renown.

Below left: Entrance to Villers-Bretonneux in 1974, with the Amiens-St. Quentin road on the right. The German front line ran across the foreground after they had been ejected from the town.

Imperial War Museum

Above: SO NEAR, YET SO FAR. The closest the Germans got to Amiens which lies 10½ miles away in the centre distance. This picture was taken from the base of Hill 104, 1¼ miles north of Villers-Bretonneux, and scene of violent actions in 1918.

Right: The Australian National War Memorial at the rear of the British cemetery on Hill 104. The memorial was designed by Sir Edward Lutyens and was unveiled by H.M. King George VI on 22nd July 1938. It perpetuates the memory of many thousands of Australian 'Missing' who have no known grave. The military cemetery contains the graves of 1,085 men from the United Kingdom, 770 Australians, 263 Canadians and several South Africans and New Zealanders.

AMIENS 1918

THE BEGINNING OF THE END

Late in May the enemy thrust forward again; by 30th he was on the banks of the Marne, and Paris, less than 60 miles away, was once more in danger. But American troops were now in the field, and two days previously the U.S. 1st Division had made history by taking Cantigny, near Montdidier. The 2nd U.S. Division, in reserve astride the main route to Paris, attacked the Germans vigorously at Chateau Thierry. On 6th June these eager though untried troops captured part of Belleau Wood, and the rest of the wood and the village of Bouresches fell to them over the next few days. Baulked, the Germans mounted another hastily prepared attack on 9th June, against the French between Noyon and Montdidier, but were stopped after advancing six miles.

Everywhere he turned, the enemy was bloodily repulsed; and on 8th August — 'the black day of the German Army', according to Ludendorff — began the Battle of Amiens, which was, without doubt, the beginning of the end.

At 4.20 a.m., in milky-white fog, thousands of Canadians, Australians and men from the United Kingdom moved forward behind massed tanks and under a curtain of covering artillery fire from over 3,000 guns. By the end of the day the Canadians had advanced as much as eight miles, losing just under 4,000 men in the process, and winning five V.C.s. The Australians had gained six or seven miles, lost 650 men, and won another V.C. The French, who had committed six divisions to the assault, had advanced five miles on the right of the Canadians, and the British flanking corps two miles. Even the cavalry had had a field day. On 8th August alone, practically five German divisions were destroyed — the greatest enemy defeat since the beginning of the war.

But in spite of this decisive victory, which became the turning point of the Allies' fortunes, the fighting dragged on, and fierce engagements continued as the enemy was forced slowly back towards the old Somme battlefields of 1916. Steadily the towns and villages captured during the March offensive were reclaimed

Imperial War Museum

Above: A daylight patrol of the London Irish Rifles moving under a damaged railway bridge on the outskirts of Albert, August 1918. The Germans were still in the town and, of this original patrol of seven men, one was killed and three wounded. Albert was recaptured on 22nd August.

by the Allies, and the seeds of demoralisation took deeper root in the minds of German soldiers.

Albert fell on 22nd August, and Thiepval and Pozières, those places of evil memory, followed. At Bapaume the New Zealanders met with strong resistance, as did the Australians in front of Péronne, before these towns were recaptured. All along the front the advance of our forces continued; while in the south the French also moved forward, though more slowly.

And so the time came when our troops were beyond the area with which this book is concerned. Once again the devastated acres over which our men had fought at such a bitter cost in 1916 and 1917, and had endeavoured to hold in March 1918, were behind our lines. Much fighting remained to be done though, and many more deaths were to occur before the guns finally fell silent. The Hindenburg Line had still to be forced, and other strong defences had yet to be overcome. Nevertheless the end was drawing nearer, and now it was mainly a question of time before the enemy collapsed.

Above left: The key position of Mont St. Quentin, just north of Pèronne, 3rd October 1918. Savage fighting took place here for two days before this fortress village, which barred the way to the town, fell to the 2nd Australian Division on September 1st. Deep shelters, connected by subterranean galleries pierced the hill, and observation posts commanded an excellent view of the countryside for miles around.

Below left: Mont St. Quentin July 1973.

Below right: Battle of St. Quentin Canal. Americans moving forward with 8th Bn. tanks, near Bellicourt, 29th September 1918. These men of the American 30th Division (which, together with the U.S. 27th Division formed the American II Corps) worked in close conjunction with the Australians at that time. Both U.S. formations fought hard, and suffered severe casualties from machine-gun fire. The 30th Division was successful in the capture of the strongly fortified southern entrance to the St. Quentin Canal.

SOMME HARVEST

Military cemeteries containing the graves of some of the very many thousands who gave their lives for that comparatively limited area of tortured ground in Picardy. British graves near Serre.

French graves near St. Quentin.

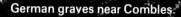
German graves near Combles.

The town of Albert seen from the north-east. The Church of Nôtre-Dame-de-Brebière is in the centre, with the Hôtel de Ville and main square below.

The Lochnagar crater viewed from the south, with La Boisselle and 'The Glory Hole' at the top.

La Boisselle looking north-west. The 'Glory Hole' crater is at centre left and the now filled-in 'Y Sap' crater at right centre.

The village of Ovillers viewed from the south. The church is in the lower centre of the photograph, with the Military Cemetery on the far left.

A slightly different view of Ovillers, again looking north, showing the Leipzig Salient area at centre right, with the Lonsdale Military Cemetery top left and Thiepval Memorial top right.

The infamous Schwaben Redoubt, looking north. The Ulster Memorial and Mill Road Cemetery is in the centre with, top left to right; Connaught Military Cemetery and Thiepval Wood; Hamel and Newfoundland Memorial Park.

The village of Aveluy, looking eastwards in the direction of Ovillers and La Boisselle.

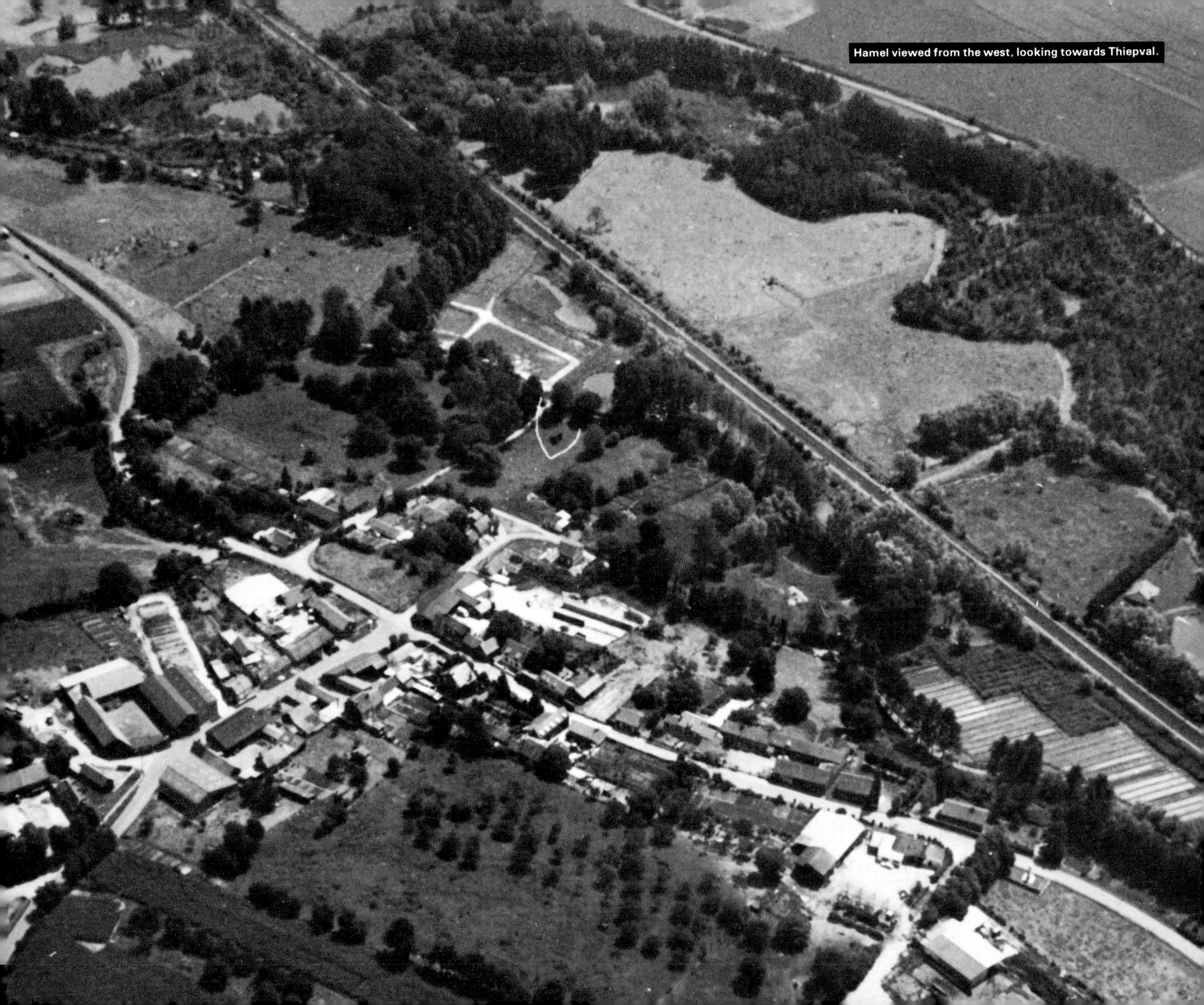

Hamel viewed from the west, looking towards Thiepval.

Pozières looking south-west. The Albert-Bapaume Road traverses the photograph with Ovillers at the top and La Boisselle in the top left-hand corner.

Courcelette, looking north-west. The Regina Trench Military Cemetery is at the top right, with Grandcourt top centre.

Martinpuich, looking north-east with the village of Le Sars upper left.

A peaceful High Wood, viewed from the south-west with Martinpuich at the top of the picture.

The notorious Butte de Warlencourt, looking north-east with the village of Warlencourt-Ecourt at the top right of the picture.

The courage and the carnage of the Somme. Seventy years ago this now peaceful countryside was a field of battle on which more than a million men became casualties — etching the name indelibly on the history of mankind.

Warlencourt-Ecourt, centre, with Pys, upper left, and Bapaume Road Military Cemetery in the foreground.

ACKNOWLEDGEMENTS

In the preparation of this book I readily received co-operation from a variety of sources connected with material used in its compilation. I am particularly indebted to the Imperial War Museum, London, as the source of wartime photographs, with special thanks to the staff of the Department of Photographs for help willingly given at all times.

Set out below are details of others who have rendered valuable assistance which is gratefully acknowledged. For the sake of simplicity names have been placed in alphabetical order:

A.P.B. International, London.	Permission to reproduce poem, 'A Death in Hospital', from "Passchendaele and The Somme", by Hugh Quigley: published by Methuen & Co. Ltd. (1928) — page 121
Mrs. Suzanne Bloxam, Lympne, Hythe, Kent.	Letters and other items connected with her father, the late Major G. F. Farran, Royal Artillery — pages xii and 78, 79
Mr. H. A. Boyce Deal, Kent.	Reminiscence relating to High Wood — page 77
Bradford Pals Association, Bradford, Yorkshire.	Details for section 'A Day to Remember' — page 9. Appreciation is expressed to Mr. G. H. Taylor, M.C., M.M., for his contribution, and special thanks are recorded for the valuable assistance given by the late Mr. Sydney Booth.
Mr. W. J. Bradley, Cheam, Surrey.	Extracts from his diary, "2nd Battalion Memories (H.A.C. Infantry)" — pages 15 and 117
Mr. C. E. Carrington, London.	Extracts from his book, "A Subaltern's War", written under the pseudonym of 'Charles Edmunds' published by Peter Davies Ltd. (1928) — pages 28, 30, 32, 119
Mr. W. F. Chapman, Ewell, Surrey.	Reminiscence relating to Flers — page 100
Chatto & Windus Ltd., London.	Extracts from "The Storm Of Steel", by Ernst Junger: published by Chatto & Windus (1929) — pages 89-91, 107, 108
Commonwealth War Graves Commission, Maidenhead.	Photograph, Blighty Valley Military Cemetery — page 25
Madame Stella Rabatel Goullieux Dargis, Paris.	Details and photograph relating to Pozières immediately after the 1914-1918 war — page 83
Faber and Faber Ltd., London.	Extracts from "Memoirs Of An Infantry Officer", by Siegfried Sassoon; published by Faber and Faber Ltd. (1930) — pages 40, 41, 43, 47, 52, 117
Llewelyn Wyn Griffith Esq	Extracts from his book "Up To Mametz": published by Faber and Faber Ltd. (1931) — pages 48, 54, 57, 59
The Controller, Her Majesty's Stationery Office, London	Permission to quote statistics and other details from "The Official History Of The War, Military Operations, France and Belgium 1916, 1917 and 1918: published (in separate volumes) by MacMillan Co. Ltd., London. Also for permission to reproduce sketch maps on pages ix, xi, xiv, 3 10, 20, 26, 42, 66, 92, 120, 124, 130, 132
Hutchinson Publishing Group Ltd., London.	Extracts from "Somme Harvest", by Giles Eyre: published by Jarrolds (Publishers) London Ltd. (1938) — pages viii, x, 11, 29, 34, 36, 55, 65, 88, 101
	Extracts from "Warrior", by Lieut.-Col. Graham Seton Hutchison, D.S.O., M.C.: published by Hutchinson & Co. (Publishers) Ltd. (1932) — pages 76, 95, 121
	Extracts from "Stand To — A Diary Of The Trenches", by Capt. F. C. Hitchcock, M.C., F.R. HIST. S.: published by Hurst & Blackett (1937), reprinted by Cedric Chivers Ltd., Bath (1975) — pages 49, 64, 86
A. D. Peters & Co., London.	Permission to reprint poem "The Ancre At Hamel — Afterwards", by Edmund Blunden: published by Oxford University Press (R. Cobden-Sanderson Ltd.), (1928) — page 18.
Sidgewick & Jackson Ltd., London.	Permission to reprint extract from poem "The Dead", by Rupert Brooke — page 122.
Anthony Sheil Associates Ltd., London.	Extracts from "A Frenchman in Khaki", by Paul Maze published by William Heinemann Ltd. (1934) — pages 35, 81, 82, 84, 109.
South African Embassy, The Director, Department of Information, London.	Story "Delville Wood" extracted from the magazine 'Report from South Africa' dated July 1966 — pages 69-73.
J. Swettenham Esq., Senior Historian at the Canadian War Museum, Ottawa.	Extract (page 103) and official historian's quotation (page 104) taken from his original article 'The Battle Of The Somme' in 'The Legionary', September 1966.
West of England Press Publishers Ltd., Tavistock, Devon.	Permission for the reproduction of two maps extracted from 'The Army Quarterly' Vols. 9 and 11. (With thanks also to Messrs. Wm. Clowes & Son, London.) — pages 58, 68.

In addition to the previous acknowledgements I wish to record thanks to the following for other assistance given:

Comte Jacques d'Alcantara de Querrieu, near Amiens, France.
W. R. Lancaster Esq., Director Australian War Memorial, Canberra City ACT.
Lorne Manchester Esq., Managing Editor of 'Legion', the national magazine of the Royal Canadian Legion, Ottawa, Canada.
W. G. Osmond Esq., State Secretary, The Returned Services League of Australia, Darlinghurst, New South Wales.
Oxford University Press Ltd., London.
Dr. A. Caenepeel, Ypres, Belgium.
Mr. Bill Dunkow, former District Branch Secretary, The Royal British Legion, Arras, France.
Col. G. B. Jarrett, O.B.E., Ret'd, Maryland, U.S.A.
Herr Regel, Bundesarchiv, Koblenz, Germany.
Monsieur and Madame J. Vassal, Albert (Somme), France.
Also:
Messrs. Basil Kidd, W. A. Johnson, Ben May (Canterbury, Kent), J. R. Nettleton, Charles Williams, M. Waterton.
Most of the typing was done by three ladies, Mrs. P. Dixon, Mrs. Anne Driscoll and Miss Joyce Boursnell, for whose help I am most grateful.
A special 'thank you' is given to Ms. Mary Freeman and Mr. Guy Swayland for services rendered.
Finally, I cannot complete the acknowledgements without paying a tribute to my wife, who, as with my previous book, regularly accompanied me to the battlefields and assisted me in many ways. Her tolerance and support helped greatly towards the completion of this work.